Summer
Devotional

Ruth Gregg

O&U
Onwards & Upwards

Onwards and Upwards Publishers

3 Radfords Turf, Cranbrook, Exeter,
EX5 7DX, United Kingdom.
www.onwardsandupwards.org

First edition, published in the United Kingdom by Onwards and Upwards Publishers (2020).

ISBN: 978-1-78815-540-3
Typeface: Sabon LT
Graphic design: LM Graphic Design

Every effort has been made by the author to obtain the necessary permissions to reproduce copyrighted material. If, however, there have been any omissions or errors, please contact the publisher to have these corrected in future reprints and editions.

The views and opinions expressed in this book are the author's own, and do not necessarily represent the views and opinions of Onwards and Upwards Publishers or its staff.

Endorsements

Times of Refreshing does what it says on the tin – it is full to overflowing with spiritual refreshment. At a time when spiritual attentiveness and soul care can be such easily neglected spiritual disciplines, due to the busy demands made on our lives by so many other things, this spiritually anointed and biblically literate gem of Ruth's is pure gold. It is a collection of inspiring and deeply personal devotionals which come out of a heart which has been captivated by the Father's amazing love and longs for deep personal and national revival – you will certainly meet the Saviour in its pages.

Rev. Daniel Kane
West Presbyterian Church, Ballymena

There are often times in the normal day-to-day hectic schedule of ministry life that you run out of steam and need to have a pit-stop. Sadly, I am on first name terms with a lot of the deli-counter staff and hot food staff all over Ballymena! This also can be said of our walk with God; we can run out of steam and need a pit-stop. In *Times of Refreshing*, Ruth has provided the perfect spiritual pick-me-up – a devotional that can allow us to pause, rest for a while, have a spiritual snack and re-charge our batteries. Better than any meal deal, *Times of Refreshing* will help us run our race and fight our battles. In fact, why don't you get your copy and keep it where you work and make it part of your daily pit-stop routine? Ruth, thank you for this gift. My prayer, like yours, is that many will find essential daily spiritual refreshing as they use *Times of Refreshing*.

Rev. Mark McConnell
Rector, Ballymena Parish Church

There is nothing quite as good for any of us as to spend the first part of the day meditating on the Word of God. As I have read through this beautiful devotional that Ruth has written, I know that many lives will be refreshed and encouraged. Ruth has brought fresh revelation on the Scriptures and nuggets of truth that you can ponder on throughout the day. I highly recommend this book as a tool for anyone who hungers for more of God.

Pastor Roy Stewart
Pastor, Celebration House, Ballymena

About the Author

 Ruth has been involved in ministry for the past thirty years. She holds a B.D. from Queens University, a Doctorate in Biblical Studies from CLU, has released various print publications, and currently resides in County Antrim, Northern Ireland. She is director of Impact Unlimited Bible College and CTTW, a 24/7 global prayer initiative.

Her passion is to inspire others through writing in a way that is insightful, meaningful and relevant. In the *Times of Refreshing* devotionals, she taps into her experiences as a pastor, teacher, wife and mother of two, to relate poignant stories from real-life experiences.

To contact the author, please write to:

Ruth Gregg
c/o Onwards and Upwards Publishers Ltd.
4 The Old Smithy
London Road
Rockbeare
EX5 2EA

More information about the author can be found on the author's web page:

www.onwardsandupwards.org/ruth-gregg

Foreword by Tommy Stewart

Times of Refreshing is a devotional full of life-changing words of inspiration and encouragement written by Dr Ruth Gregg, drawn from a lifetime of study of God's Word. The devotional has been written to encourage the reader to trust God in every circumstance of life and to give the reader courage each day to step out in faith, believing that God is with them and has good plans for their lives.

I have known Dr Ruth Gregg from our college days when Ruth was studying Theology and I was studying Economics. My earliest impressions were of someone deeply committed to the study of God's Word and to being able to communicate it in such a way that the Word of God came alive in the life of the hearer. Through Ruth's ministry, both as a pastor and a teacher, she has shown herself to be "a worker who does not need to be ashamed and who correctly handles the Word of truth" (2 Tim. 2:15). Her dedication to creating teaching materials for pastors in the 10/40 window and her passion for revival mean that Ruth's writings are filled with great truths, anointed by the Holy Spirit.

If, like me, you have struggled to read and meditate daily on what the Bible has to say, then *Times of Refreshing* will provide you with the opportunity to develop a daily rhythm of reading and mediating on the truth of God's Word.

It is said that it takes twenty-one days to develop a habit. I can think of few better habits that you could develop than creating space each day, with the help of *Times of Refreshing*, to be refreshed by God's Word.

I wonder, can you answer yes to any of the following questions?

- Do you want to have a deeper sense of God's peace?
- Do you want to grow closer to God?
- Do you want to be more like Jesus?
- Do you want to know more of God's Word?
- Do you want to grow in confidence in who you are in Christ?

Then, be assured, *Times of Refreshing* is for you!

Tommy Stewart
Founder/Director, Christians Who Lead

June

June

1

The Simple Bare Necessities

For by grace you have been saved through faith ... it is the gift of God.

Ephesians 2:8 (NKJV)

We are great at complicating life. For example, try reading the sentence, "All the faith he had had had had no effect on the outcome of his life." While it may look like someone copied "had" and pressed the paste button a few too many times, this is actually an example of what happens when the past perfect tense gets used back-to-back. The first and third "had" are the auxiliary verbs, while the second and fourth ones are the main verbs. Stylistically speaking, the sentence would probably be less confusing if written, "He had had a lot of faith, but it had had no effect on the outcome of his life," but what fun is that?

How I loved *The Jungle Book* as a child. It was a thrilling, adventure-filled journey with the boy Mowgli as he made his way to the man-village with Bagheera, the wise panther. Along the way he met the bear Baloo, who taught Mowgli the catchy song, *The Bare Necessities* (of life). The opening lines state, "Look for the bare necessities, the simple bare necessities." I was thinking of this as I read Ephesians 2:8 which gives us the simple bare necessities of salvation.

Pay close attention to ten single-syllable words: "by grace ... through faith ... it is the gift of God."

One of the outstanding aspects of the gospel is its simplicity. As Charles Haddon Spurgeon said:

God be thanked for the simplicity of the gospel.

Jesus said, again in single syllable words:

And ye shall know the truth, and the truth shall make you free.

John 8:32 (KJV)

Don't complicate what God made simple. Paul warned:

> *But I fear, lest by any means, as the serpent beguiled Eve through his subtlety, so your minds should be corrupted from the simplicity that is in Christ.*
>
> *2 Corinthians 11:3 (KJV)*

Are we getting side-tracked by the superficial and secondary? Do we need to return to the main menu: the exquisite simplicity of the gospel? By grace... through faith... it is the gift of God.

2

Feedback Time

Now when Jesus came into the district of Caesarea Philippi,
He was asking His disciples, "Who do people say that the Son
of Man is?" And they said, "Some say John the Baptist; and
others, Elijah; but still others, Jeremiah, or one of the
prophets." He said to them, "But who do you say that I am?"
Simon Peter answered, "You are the Christ, the Son of the
living God." And Jesus said to him, "Blessed are you, Simon
Barjona, because flesh and blood did not reveal this to you,
but My Father who is in heaven."

Matthew 16:13-17 (NASB)

The Hawaiian alphabet has 13 letters. The Cambodian alphabet has 74 letters. The English alphabet has 26 letters. A sentence which contains all 26 letters of the English alphabet is called a pangram. A famous pangram is, "The quick brown fox jumps over the lazy dog." If you were to write out every number name in full (one, two, three, four...), you wouldn't use a single letter B until you reached one billion. The longest English word that can be spelled without repeating any letters is 'uncopyrightable'. The longest English word with its letters in reverse alphabetical order is 'spoonfeed'. The shortest word in the English language that contains the letters: abcdef is 'feedback'.

Feedback. As Jesus came to the region of Caesarea Philippi, He asked the question, "Who do people say that I am?" This is one of the most probing questions in the whole of the New Testament. Jesus asked for feedback from the people. Some of the disciples replied, "John the Baptist." Others said, "Elijah," or, "One of the prophets." Jesus persisted with a more personal question: "But who do *you* say that I am?" The structure of this question in Greek emphasises the word 'you'. It could be translated more literally, "And you, who do you say that I am?" Only Simon Peter ventured a reply: "Thou art the Christ."[1]

If Jesus were to look you in the eye today and say, "Who do you say that I am?" what would your answer be? Are you still listening to the rumours of culture? I hope your answer is like the disciple Peter who said, "You are the Christ, the Son of the Living God." Our answer to that question has the potential to influence our lives, our eternities. It changes why we get up, why we go to work, why we serve, why we manage our money the way we do, why we love our families the way we do, and why we live our lives. Feedback time: *who is Jesus to you?*

---

[1]   Mark 8:29 (KJV)

3

An Excellent Spirit

Then this Daniel distinguished himself above the governors and satraps, because an excellent spirit was in him; and the king gave thought to setting him over the whole realm.

Daniel 6:3 (NKJV)

id you know:

- The average golf ball has 336 dimples.
- The average bed contains over 6 billion dust mites.
- The average hen lays 228 eggs a year.
- The average porcupine has 30,000 spikes.
- The average cow produces 40 glasses of milk a day.
- On average there are 8 peas in a pod.
- The average mature oak tree sheds over 700,000 leaves in autumn.

A.W. Tozer, the noted theologian, wrote:

Refuse to be average. Let your heart soar as high as it will.

It's interesting and important to note that the word 'average' is not in the King James Version, New King James, New International, New American Standard, Amplified or New Living Translation of the Bible. It isn't in any of those translations because God created, empowered and destined each of us to rise above average – to move into excellence in all that we do.

Consider the account of Daniel. The word "excellent" in today's reading means 'to go beyond the norm, to break out of the status quo, to exceed the common measure, to surpass'. Like Daniel, we are to distinguish ourselves by God's empowering presence in our lives. Reading through the book of Daniel you see that he was a man of purpose.

Daniel purposed in his heart that he would not defile himself.

Daniel 1:8 (KJV)

He allowed God's Word to shape the attitudes of his heart and boundaries of his behaviour right from the beginning. He was also a man of prayer.

> *He went home and knelt down as usual in his upstairs room, with its windows open toward Jerusalem. He prayed three times a day, just as he had always done, giving thanks to his God.*
>
> *Daniel 6:10 (NLT)*

Notice this verse says that Daniel prayed before the Lord "just as he had always done".

These are only two examples of excellence in Daniel's life. Don't fall into the 'average Christian' category. You have a high calling.

> *I press toward the mark for the prize of the high calling of God in Christ Jesus.*
>
> *Philippians 3:14 (KJV)*

The world is already filled with mediocrity, so don't settle for adding more white noise. Refuse to be average.

4

The Red in Redemption

Come now, let us reason together, says the LORD: though your
sins are like scarlet, they shall be as white as snow; though
they are red like crimson, they shall become like wool.

Isaiah 1:18 (ESV)

From the primary colours of red, yellow and blue, to the more complex colour mixtures around us, colour adds an aesthetic ambiance to our environment. Here are some not-so-common colour facts:

- At birth Dalmatian dogs are always white.
- The safest car colour is white.
- Mosquitoes prefer children to adults and blondes to brunettes.
- The colour of a chilli pepper is no indication of its heat (usually, the smaller, the hotter).
- The most popular toothbrush colour is blue.
- The 'black box' that houses an airplane's voice recorder is actually orange so it can be more easily detected amid the debris of a plane crash.

The colours red and white feature in Isaiah 1:18. The colour red in the Bible represents blood and redemption: *red* for *red*-emption. The thread of red can be traced throughout the Bible. It also represents our sin. We even talk about being caught red-handed. The words "scarlet" and "crimson" refer to dye that was extracted from both shellfish and a certain type of insect. When white garments were dyed with these colours, they could never be made white again. These colours were both colourfast and indelible. The colour white represents righteousness and purity.

The following question was asked in a science magazine:

Why does a scarlet or crimson object appear white when viewed through a red glass in the light?

The answer given was fascinating:

When a scarlet or crimson object is viewed through a red glass in the light, the object appears white. When light hits a red object, that means all visible wavelengths are being absorbed except the frequency red, which is reflected.

Our sins are washed white, or clean, through the blood of Jesus. The blood of Jesus is red, and by using red to eliminate red (representing our sin) we become white. Though our sins are as scarlet, the Father looks on them through the filter of the blood of His Son and sees us white and pure. He is able to cleanse us from all sin.

But if we walk in the light, as He is in the light, we have fellowship with one another, and the blood of Jesus, his Son, purifies us from all sin.

1 John 1:7 (NIV)

The Sovereign Lord extends to you and I the invitation to, "Come now, let us reason together." Or as another translation goes, "Come now, let us settle the matter."[2]

---

[2] NIV

5

Etch-a-Sketch

*Think of it! All sins forgiven, the slate wiped clean, that old
arrest warrant canceled and nailed to Christ's cross.*

Colossians 2:13-14 (MSG)

On January 16, 2013, Andre Cassagnes died in Paris at the age of eighty-six. The French-born inventor was in his early thirties when he created a plastic device with a glass screen on which children could draw by turning little knobs. We know it today as the Etch-A-Sketch. An Etch-A-Sketch has a thick, flat grey screen in a red plastic frame. There are two white knobs on the front of the frame in the lower corners. Twisting the knobs moves a stylus which displaces aluminium powder on the back of the screen, leaving a solid line. The knobs create lineographic images. The left control moves the stylus horizontally, and the right one moves it vertically. Turning both knobs simultaneously makes diagonal lines.

You can have so much fun, and with a little bit of practice you can actually do some very creative things with an Etch-A-Sketch. Surfing the Internet, I found people who are true Etch-A-Sketch artists and make a profession out of it. But for those of us who are amateurs at it and frequently mess up, there is something special about the Etch-A-Sketch. Shaking it covers the screen in a fresh coat of powder so the artist can start all over again. You shake it and it wipes the slate clean. In 1995, the Etch-A-Sketch toy was featured in the original film *Toy Story*, in a scene where one toy performs a 'quick draw' duel with Woody. This twelve-second feature was enough to give a significant sales boost, requiring the production line to work overtime to meet demand. It's unlikely that André Cassagnes had any idea the toy he created in his basement well over half a century ago would become so popular. It's also unlikely that he imagined his hand-held creation would also provide Christians with such a powerful illustration of grace.

I am so thankful we have an Etch-A-Sketch kind of God. When I take all my mistakes, my sins, my bad decisions and my failures to Him, He wipes the slate clean. That's what we are told in Colossians 2. And again, in Hebrews 10:17, God says:

I'll forever wipe the slate clean of their sins.

Hebrews 10:17 (MSG)

Our slate, covered with a lifetime's records of sin, is wiped clean for eternity. Meditate on what the Psalmist realised:

If You kept a record of our sins, who could escape being condemned? But You forgive us, so that we should stand in awe of You.

Psalm 130:3-4 (GNB)

6

Finding Me in Nemo

"Suppose one of you has a hundred sheep and loses one of them. Doesn't he leave the ninety-nine in the open country and go after the lost sheep until he finds it? And when he finds it, he joyfully puts it on his shoulders and goes home. Then he calls his friends and neighbors together and says, 'Rejoice with me; I have found my lost sheep.'"

Luke 15:4-6 (NIV)

One of the joys of visiting the dentist was being given a *Finding Nemo* sticker as an award for bravery! It was one of those "I was brave for the dentist" occasions. *Finding Nemo* was one of the Blockbuster movies released by Pixar Studios with great animation and wonderful characters. The film is the story of a fish, Nemo, who is captured, and his father's journey against incredible odds to save him. Nemo disobeyed his father and swam beyond his beautiful home on the Great Barrier Reef. As he swam further and further from safety, he was suddenly scooped up by a diver and taken away on a boat. Nemo's disobedience caused him to be separated from his father. He was so sad because there was nothing he could do to get back to his father. Nemo ended up in a dentist's aquarium overlooking the Sydney Harbour – less free than he would have been had he stayed at home. His situation seemed hopeless. The father loved little Nemo so much that it did not matter how big the ocean was or how many fish there were. He was determined to save him, and set out on an incredible adventure to seek and save little Nemo. This film illustrates a love of a father for his son and his commitment to never stop searching until he brings him home.

The theme in *Finding Nemo* is a great parallel of God's amazing love for his children. Just as Nemo's father risked everything to find Nemo, so our heavenly Father risked it all to find us.

> *See what great love the Father has lavished on us, that we should be called children of God! And that is what we are!*
>
> *1 John 3:1 (NIV)*

> *But God demonstrates his own love for us in this: While we were still sinners, Christ died for us.*
>
> *Romans 5:8 (NIV)*

In Luke 15 Jesus illustrated the extent of the Father's *agape* love in *The Parable of the Lost Sheep*. He showed how the shepherd would risk all to find the lost sheep and bring it home. Like Nemo we have all strayed and made wrong decisions. As a result, we were separated from our father's love. But like Nemo we also know the extent to which our Father will go to bring his lost children home. We are the recipients of His love; or, as the hymn says:

> *Wide, wide as the ocean, high as the heaven above;*
> *Deep, deep as the deepest sea is my Saviour's love.*
> *I, though so unworthy, still am a child of His care;*
> *For His Word teaches me that His love reaches me*
> * everywhere.*

7

Dress in the Wardrobe God Picked Out for You

Since God chose you to be the holy people he loves, you must clothe yourselves with tenderhearted mercy, kindness, humility, gentleness, and patience. Make allowance for each other's faults, and forgive anyone who offends you. Remember, the Lord forgave you, so you must forgive others. Above all, clothe yourselves with love, which binds us all together in perfect harmony.

Colossians 3:12-14 (NLT)

*I*t has long been said that 'clothes maketh the man'. Or, 'you are what you wear'. We have even coined the phrase 'dress to impress'. Experts have studied the intriguing science behind fashion psychology. Apparently nine out of ten women own at least one item of clothing they have never worn. Patients put more trust in a doctor who wears a white coat. The human eye takes longer to travel across patterned fabrics; this makes the body appear larger. After trying on clothing men are more than twice as likely as women to buy. Men are more likely to approach a woman for a date if she is wearing the colour red.

It's common knowledge that clothes have a strong influence over the way other people perceive us. Our style and the clothes we choose also reflect and affect our mood and overall confidence. Scientists call this phenomenon 'enclothed cognition'. Paul talked about how to dress in the wardrobe God picked out for us.

You're done with that old life. It's like a filthy set of ill-fitting clothes you've stripped off and put in the fire. Now you're dressed in a new wardrobe. Every item of your new way of life is custom-made by the Creator, with his label on it. All the old fashions are now obsolete. ... So, chosen by God for this new life of love, dress in the wardrobe God picked out for you: compassion, kindness, humility, quiet strength, discipline. Be even-tempered, content with second place, quick to forgive an offence. Forgive as quickly and completely as the Master forgave you. And regardless of what else you put on, wear love. It's your basic, all-purpose garment. Never be without it.

Colossians 3:9-10,12-14 (MSG)

God has picked out some articles of clothing that He believes are essential for every believer. Are there any items which we are not wearing? We might regularly wear the shirt of compassion, and shoes of kindness, but perhaps leave the jacket of discipline on the hanger. Kindness, humility, quiet strength and discipline never go out of fashion. Forgiveness looks great no matter what season we are in. The best part is that these clothes, unlike the ones you buy at stores, will never go out of style.

There is one all-purpose garment which God states we are never to be without. Love is the one piece of clothing we need to be wearing at all times – no matter the season, predicted weather forecast or agenda of our day. Love is the garment that coordinates and pulls the outfit together.

Have you ever seen the red carpet interviews where they ask the celebrities the question, "Who are you wearing?" They usually name some famous clothing designer, but today I would like to ask you the same question. "Who are *you* wearing?" The Book of Romans tells us:

...put on the Lord Jesus Christ.

Romans 13:14 (ESV)

The fact that Jesus is alive in us should be visible to everyone! Dress in the wardrobe God has picked out for you and reflect the beautiful qualities of Christ to the world.

8

The Power of Partnership

I thank my God every time I remember you. In all my prayers for all of you, I always pray with joy because of your partnership in the Gospel from the first day until now.

Philippians 1:3-5 (NIV)

The term 'mutualism' refers to a relationship in biology or sociology which is mutually beneficial to two living things. Many animals have developed mutually beneficial relationships with each other. "You scratch my back, and I'll scratch yours," say plenty of animals. For example, oxpeckers and zebras. Nobody likes to be covered in ticks, not even zebras. So these large mammals are happy when oxpecker birds hang out on their backs, eating the bugs and parasites which irritate their skin. The zebras are free from pesky pests, and the birds get delicious meals through a readily available source of food. Also, when there is a danger to the zebra, the oxpecker flies high and makes much noise in order to alert nearby animals to the impending danger (i.e. a predator).

Another mutually beneficial relationship is found between the clownfish and sea anemone. Clownfish live within the protective tentacles of the sea anemone. In return, the sea anemone receives cleaning and protection from the clownfish.

Paul wrote to the Philippians in 1:3, thanking God for the partnership with Philippian Christians in sharing the gospel. He emphasised the importance of partnership when he said that we are "God's fellow workers"[3]. Paul 'walked his talk' when it came to partnerships in ministry. Throughout his life, he personally demonstrated the principle of partnership and he succinctly summarised this principle when he wrote:

---

[3] 1 Corinthians 3:9 (ESV)

I planted the seed, Apollos watered it, but God has been making it grow.

1 Corinthians 3:6 (NIV)

He told us to encourage one another and build each other up on a daily basis. Live in harmony with one another. Love one another. Accept one another. Be kind and compassionate to one another, forgiving each other, just as in Christ God forgave you. Submit to one another out of reverence for Christ. Bear with each other and forgive whatever grievances you may have against one another. Spur one another on toward love and good deeds.

May our relationships with our fellow believers be mutually beneficial. May we be encouraged and be encouragers as we realise our partnership in the gospel.

9

Eyes on the Horizon

Don't shuffle along, eyes to the ground, absorbed with the things right in front of you. Look up, and be alert to what is going on around Christ – that's where the action is. See things from His perspective.

Colossians 3:1-2 (MSG)

*H*ave you ever felt seasick or suffered from *mal de mer?* In the days when I was out with my father on his fishing boat, we would sometimes hit choppy water around Garron Tower and the boat would pitch or roll. At a certain point the still waters suddenly morphed into mountains of angry waves. My face would adopt a pasty complexion and I truly felt like a miserable mariner. The advice given to me to avoid future seasickness was to focus on the horizon. "Don't look at the waves around you. Look at the horizon far away. Look at that stable, stationary line and you will feel better. Use the horizon as a point to maintain your equilibrium." Looking into the distance has long been touted as a way to stay upright and free of seasickness despite the pitch and roll of a boat. In a recently published article in a magazine called *Psychological Science,* experts found that staring at the horizon makes people steadier while at sea. "It's the people who become wobbly who subsequently become motion sick," said Thomas Stoffregen, a cognitive scientist at the University of Minnesota.

We all know that life has its fair share of ups and downs. Temporary turbulence in whatever form can be burdensome, depressing and overwhelming. In turbulent times at sea the worst thing you can do is to lock yourself in your cabin and look down. Paul realised in Colossians 3 that too many of us have a tendency to shuffle along, eyes to the ground. It's easy to get busy and absorbed with the things right in front of us and lose all sense of balance and equilibrium. We get self-absorbed in our problems. We worry too much. We stress too much. We focus on the wind-whipped waves.

To navigate turbulent times, we must stabilise ourselves by looking beyond the circumstances.

> *And set your minds and keep them set on what is above (the higher things), not on the things that are on the earth.*
>
> *Colossians 3:2 (AMPC)*

When life has got you down, look up. A sure safeguard to impede the irregular pitches of life is a continual setting of our mind upon the things above! Make this your point of reference.

10

Squirrel Antics

"Do not lay up for yourselves treasures on earth, where moth and rust destroy and where thieves break in and steal, but lay up for yourselves treasures in heaven, where neither moth nor rust destroys and where thieves do not break in and steal. For where your treasure is, there your heart will be also."

Matthew 6:19-21 (ESV)

I have been interested in squirrels ever since the days of reading *The Tale of Squirrel Nutkin* by Beatrix Potter, a story about an impertinent red squirrel who loses his tail. As cold weather approaches and food sources start to diminish, squirrels prepare by stockpiling their food. I was amazed to discover that they store up to ten thousand pine cones a year! They have also been spotted organising their nut booty by variety, quality and even by their personal preference, according to new research. This apparently is known as 'chunking'. Furthermore, they have sophisticated caching techniques, hiding their prized treats from potential pilferers. Scatter hoarding is effective, as are their acorn larders. I always wondered how they located their stashes. It's all down to their saliva which acts as an olfactory signpost.

Jesus told us to "lay up for yourselves treasures in heaven" (Matthew 6:20). In Jesus' time, the Jews to whom He was speaking would have been very familiar with the terms "earthly treasure" and "heavenly treasure". It was part of the vernacular of the time. In fact, the Jews defined storing up treasure in heaven as deeds of mercy and deeds of kindness to people in distress.

Paul instructs those who are rich...

...[not] to set their hopes on the uncertainty of riches, but on God, who richly provides us with everything to enjoy. They are to do good, to be rich in good works, to be generous and ready to share, thus storing up treasure for themselves as a

good foundation for the future, so that they may take hold of that which is truly life.

1 Timothy 6:17-19 (ESV)

Be generous and ready to share, thus storing up treasure. Where is your treasure? Is it free from the potential pilferers of moth, rust and thieves? Are we scatter hoarding for ourselves or scattering our gifts abroad, as in Psalm 112:9:

They have freely scattered their gifts to the poor, their righteousness endures forever.

Psalm 112:9 (NIV)

People say, "You can't take it with you." Jesus contradicted that adage by citing the common Jewish belief that resources given to the needy will be repaid and rewarded. Lay up for yourselves treasures in heaven. Stockpile what's valuable in God's eyes and invest in what truly matters.

11

Green Fingers

For since by man came death, by man came also the resurrection of the dead. For as in Adam all die, even so in Christ shall all be made alive.

1 Corinthians 15:21-22 (KJV)

'Green Fingers' is the term given to anyone with a natural ability in growing plants. I'm sure we all appreciate a picturesque garden whether it is in our own back yard or in a communal area. I have been blessed by always finding myself situated in close proximity to a garden. At university I was next door to the Botanic Gardens in Belfast, a beautiful Victorian heritage hosting an extensive rose garden and Palm House Conservatory. While living in County Kildare, the world-famous Japanese Gardens were near-at-hand. The vibrant colours of the Japanese maples interspersed with plants which evoked the exotic. Now I'm back north, and convenient to the Antrim Castle Gardens where many blossoms perfume the air. Many towns and villages around here compete annually in an *Ulster in Bloom* competition, seeing reward for their horticultural achievement, environmental responsibility and community participation.

The Bible features gardens of even more importance. Man was created in the beginning and placed in a garden: the Garden of Eden.

And the Lord God planted a garden eastward in Eden, and there He put the man whom He had formed.

Genesis 2:8 (GNB)

God created man to have a relationship and walked in the garden with Adam and Eve. The name "Eden" means 'pleasantness', and since everything the Lord had made was "very good"[4], the Garden of Eden must have been a delightful place. However, we associate this garden

---

[4]   Genesis 1:31 (NIV)

with sin as man's relationship with God was broken there. No longer would Adam and Eve enjoy a flawless environment. The story of this first garden is a story that reminds us that even though we can see glimpses of God's beauty and presence in creation today, it is also a world that is filled with sin and brokenness.

There is another garden, the Garden of Gethsemane, which we associate with suffering as Jesus agonised in prayer prior to Calvary. We read in Matthew:

> *...[He] began to be sorrowful and very heavy.*
>
> *Matthew 26:37 (KJV)*

The word Gethsemane means 'place of the olive press' and that perfectly describes those crushing hours of Christ's suffering on our behalf.

> *...in anguish, he prayed ... and his sweat was like drops of blood falling to the ground.*
>
> *Luke 22:44 (NIV)*

Three times Jesus prayed that if it were possible, the cup of suffering would be taken from Him, but that the will of the Father would nevertheless be done.

There is also the Garden of Golgotha of which John writes:

> *Now in the place where He was crucified there was a garden, and in the garden a new tomb in which no one had yet been laid.*
>
> *John 19:41 (ESV)*

This was the garden where Jesus was laid in a tomb. Early in the morning, while it was still dark, at least five women set out with spices to visit the tomb in which Jesus had been buried.[5]

When they arrived, they discovered that the massive stone had been rolled away from the opening of the tomb and that the body was no longer in the tomb. Jesus asked Mary why she was weeping. And notice what the Gospel writer, John, says next. His detail is very important.

> *Supposing him to be the gardener...*
>
> *John 20:15 (ESV)*

---

[5] See Luke 24:1

Mary thought that Jesus was a gardener because, after all, this was a garden tomb. In a way, Mary was right. Jesus is a gardener, because it would be by his death and resurrection that the thorns and the thistles of God's good creation would finally be removed forever.

The first Adam sinned in a garden; the last Adam took this sin upon Himself. In one garden Adam took a fall. In another Jesus took a stand. He suffered and died to take away "the sin of the world"[6] and restore our broken relationship with God. Let's learn from these gardens, appreciating the lessons from each.

---

[6] John 1:29 (NIV)

12

A Well-Watered Garden

The LORD will guide you always;
he will satisfy your needs in a sun-scorched land
and will strengthen your frame.
You will be like a well-watered garden,
like a spring whose waters never fail.

Isaiah 58:11 (NIV)

Google "the secrets of a good garden" and you will find the following need attention:

Soil: An important ingredient of growing a garden is the proper preparation of the soil. One of the biggest factors when it comes to healthy soil is its pH because if the soil is too acidic or too alkaline then your plants will have a much harder time growing and getting nutrients from the soil. If you know that your soil is too acidic, for example, then you can add lime to the soil to help balance the pH. In the parable of the sower Jesus identified four types of soil which are worth studying and applying.[7] Hosea also reminds us:

Break up your fallow ground,
For it is time to seek the LORD
Until He comes to rain righteousness on you.

Hosea 10:12 (NASB)

Weeds: From the very beginning, weeds have been a symbol of mankind's disobedience to God. Weeds choke plants, creating an atmosphere where growth can be impossible. In Jesus' parable, weeds, identified as the cares of life, rose up and choked the seedlings before they could bear fruit.

---

[7]　See Mark 4

And others fell among the thorns, and the thorns came up and choked them out.

Mark 4:7 (NASB)

They will overtake us unless their roots are yanked.

Light: Any experienced gardener will tell you that sunshine is essential for the growth of plants. Plants grow towards the light. Through the process of photosynthesis, plants draw energy directly from the sun and store that energy in the form of fruit. The Scripture says that God is light[8] and we are to walk in the light. We cannot expect to be fruitful if we live in darkness.

Pruning: Pruning is essential in maintaining the health and fruit-bearing ability of any plant or tree. God prunes away those things in our lives that have become old and useless. Sometimes that pruning is the removal of our 'old ways' of the world. By so doing, the Lord knows that we will grow healthier, and stronger.

"I am the true vine, and my Father is the gardener. He cuts off every branch in me that bears no fruit, while every branch that does bear fruit he prunes so that it will be even more fruitful."

John 15:1-2 (NIV)

Water: Water is the most important thing we have been given by God to support our life system. We can go many days without food and live, but without water, we will be dead in a few short days. Water is a key element in growing a garden. Both seeds and plants need adequate moisture to grow. Water is symbolic of the Word of God. Isaiah said:

"As the rain and the snow come down from heaven, and do not return to it without watering the earth and making it bud and flourish, so that it yields seed for the sower and bread for the eater, so is my word that goes out from my mouth: It will not return to me empty, but will accomplish what I desire and achieve the purpose for which I sent it."

Isaiah 55:10 (NIV)

You will be like a well-watered garden. How is your garden looking today? The best way to grow a lush and healthy garden is to keep it under the care of the master gardener.

---

[8]   See 1 John 1:5

13

A Confectionery Conundrum

"How long will you waver between two opinions? If the LORD is God, follow Him…"

1 Kings 18:21 (NIV)

*H*ow would you describe a Jaffa Cake to someone who has never eaten one? It's a delicious circular configuration consisting of a small sponge with an indulgent dark chocolate cap covering a veneer of orange jelly. Named after Jaffa oranges, the Jaffa Cake was invented as a small cake by McVitie's back in the 1920s. The confectionery conundrum which still persists to this day is this: are Jaffa Cakes actually cakes or biscuits? After a court ruling in 1991, they were deemed as cakes. Apparently, a tax is charged on chocolate-covered biscuits but not on cakes. The manufacturer, McVitie's, had always categorised them as cakes and to boost their revenue the tax authorities wanted them recategorised as biscuits. Happily for us Jaffa Cake lovers who would not relish the prospect of having to pay another 17.5% for our Jaffa Cakes, the court ruled in favour of McVitie's. You can imagine why there were howls of derision when the Jaffa Cake was named Britain's fifth favourite biscuit! It looks like a biscuit, it's shaped like a biscuit and it's packaged like a biscuit, so why is a Jaffa Cake classified as a cake? The court found, as anyone who has forgotten to put the lid on their biscuit tin properly will know, that when biscuits go stale, they go softer. But when cakes go stale, they go harder. The test was done, and when Jaffa cakes were left exposed to the air, they got harder. Yet you still find them in the biscuit aisle next to custard creams and bourbons. They straddle the two worlds of moist cake produce and crunchy biscuits.

In Christianity you cannot straddle the fence. You can't be 50% Christian and 50% worldly. Elijah challenged the people to stop straddling the fence and make a choice. "How long will you waver between two opinions?"[9] he asked. The Bible uses the term "lukewarm" to describe someone straddling the fence of Christianity. Jesus says to a church in Revelation:

> *"I know your works: you are neither cold nor hot. Would that you were either cold or hot! So, because you are lukewarm, and neither hot nor cold, I will spit you out of my mouth."*
>
> *Revelation 3:15-16 (ESV)*

Jesus also taught us:

> *No man can serve two masters: for either he will hate the one, and love the other; or else he will hold to the one, and despise the other.*
>
> *Matthew 6:24; Luke 16:13 (KJV)*

James phrased it this way:

> *You adulterous people! Do you not know that friendship with the world is enmity with God? Therefore whoever wishes to be a friend of the world makes himself an enemy of God.*
>
> *James 4:4 (ESV)*

Have you ever seen someone with one foot on the edge of a boat and the other on the dock? As the boat begins to drift away from the dock, the person can't decide whether to get onto the boat or the dock, and in the moment of indecision, they end up in the lake. Are we fully following the Lord, or are we also wavering between two opinions? If we are wavering, or lukewarm, then it is time to make a decision. Will you, will I, fully follow the Lord? He is God, who loves us, cares for us, has all wisdom and power and so the invitation is before us: "If the Lord is God, follow Him!"

---

[9]   1 Kings 18:21 (NIV)

14

30 Pieces of Silver

Then one of the twelve, who was called Judas Iscariot, went to the chief priests and said, "What will you give me if I deliver him to you?" And they paid him thirty pieces of silver. And from that moment he sought an opportunity to betray him.

Matthew 26:14-16

When a person mentions thirty pieces of silver, many immediately think of Judas' betrayal of Jesus, so familiar is his betrayal etched in our memories. To be a 'Judas' has long been part of Western culture's portrayal of betrayal. When Matthew comes to list the names of the apostles he begins with Peter, James and John, and then the others. Judas is last – always. But never just Judas but "Judas ... who betrayed him"[10]. When Mark writes his Gospel it is the same: "Judas who betrayed him". When Luke writes his gospel, it is the same: "Judas who betrayed him". Then thirty years after that, John – by now in his 80s or 90s – writes his Gospel. He calls him "Judas ... who was later to betray him"[11].

The chief rulers found that thirty pieces of silver were sufficient money to buy the betrayal of Jesus into their hands. In Hebrew culture, thirty pieces of silver was not a lot of money. In fact, it was the exact price paid to the master of a slave if and when his slave was gored by an ox:

But if the ox gores a slave, either male or female, the animal's owner must pay the slave's owner thirty silver coins, and the ox must be stoned.

Exodus 21:32 (NLT)

The slave's death was compensated by the thirty pieces of silver.

---

[10] Matthew 10:4 (NIV)
[11] John 12:4 (NIV)

Jesus redeemed us from the slave market of sin – that's the doctrine of redemption. Redemption is Jesus Christ paying a price we could never pay to deliver us from our bondage to sin through His death on the cross. God did not purchase our freedom with gold or silver, the typical currency for buying human slaves, but with the blood of His beloved Son. As the Bible says:

> *Ye know that ye were not redeemed with corruptible things, as silver and gold, from your vain conversation ... But with the precious blood of Christ, as of a lamb without blemish and without spot.*
>
> *1 Peter 1:18-19 (KJV)*

Judas returned the thirty pieces of silver to the chief priests and elders, saying, "I have sinned in betraying innocent blood."[12] Every word was true. With remorse, he threw the money back into the temple, the coins clinking and ringing as they hit the stone pavement. As Judas turned to go, the thirty pieces of silver stayed behind. The Jews saw this as blood money and they couldn't use it in the temple so they ended up buying the potter's field,[13] foretold by Zechariah hundreds of years earlier. In addition, the prophet Jeremiah had prophesied about this long ago,[14] as noted by Matthew when he wrote:

> *Then was fulfilled what had been spoken by the prophet Jeremiah, saying, "And they took the thirty pieces of silver, the price of him on whom a price had been set by some of the sons of Israel, and they gave them for the potter's field, as the Lord directed me."*
>
> *Matthew 27:9-10 (ESV)*

Judas is a sad illustration of the Bible's warning, "The heart is deceitful above all things, and desperately wicked; who can know it?"[15] May we learn from his tragic example and remain steadfast in our commitment to Jesus.

---

[12] Matthew 27:4 (AMPC)
[13] See Matthew 27:7
[14] See Jeremiah 19:1,6,11
[15] Jeremiah 17:9 (NKJV)

15

1:21 or 2:21?

For to me to live is Christ, and to die is gain.

Philippians 1:21 (KJV)

*T*his is very personal for Paul: "For *to me...*" Regardless of how anyone else is living, he is saying, "For *to me...*" Notice how he ends the phrase: "...is Christ." Literally, in the original Greek in which this is written, the verb "is" is not found. It is applied by our translators just to smooth it out, but literally, in dramatic effect, this reads, as Paul penned it, "For me to live, Christ." We live *in* Christ... *for* Christ... *by* Christ... *through* Christ. *For me to live, Christ.*

To the Colossians, Paul says in rich expression:

Christ is our life.

Colossians 3:4 (NLV)

For Paul, "to live" was wrapped up in Christ. He had no competing loyalties. No other agenda. The entire reason for his life, the entire reason for which Paul preached, travelled and even suffered persecution can be reduced to this one word, "Christ". Everything in his life must be brought into alignment with the chief cornerstone, Christ. Everything had to square with Christ. It reminds me of the song, "Jesus, all for Jesus, all I am and have, and ever hope to be."[16]

Surely this verse from Paul challenges us to consider our own statement of faith. "To me to live is _____." What word or phrase would you put in the blank? Is Christ your purpose? Is Christ your passion? Is Christ your priority?

The opposite of this single-minded focus is found in the following verse:

---

[16] Robin Mark; *Jesus, All for Jesus;* from the album *Revival in Belfast* (1999)

For they all seek after their own interests, not those of Christ Jesus.

Philippians 2:21 (NASB)

We are living in a 'me generation'. A selfie generation. Most people are interested in themselves, their advancement, their concerns. Or as Paul put it, "...they all seek after their own interests..." Paul wrote to Timothy as a warning:

But understand this, that in the last days there will come times of difficulty. For people will be lovers of self.

2 Timothy 3:1-2 (ESV)

They all seek after their own interests, yet Jesus has told us to "seek first" something else.

"But seek first the kingdom of God and His righteousness, and all these things shall be added to you."

Matthew 6:33 (ESV)

Paul stated:

He died for all, that those who live should live no longer for themselves, but for Him who died for them and rose again.

2 Corinthians 5:15 (NKJV)

How tragic that we can easily become intoxicated with 'love for self' rather than 'death of self', turning God's truth completely on its head.

The challenge remains: are we Christ-centred life or self-centred? Would Philippians 1:21 or Philippians 2:21 best describe us?

16

The Two-Four Factor

Do nothing from selfish ambition or conceit, but in humility count others more significant than yourselves. Let each of you look not only to his own interests, but also to the interests of others. Have this mind among yourselves, which is yours in Christ Jesus.

Philippians 2:3-5 (ESV)

*T*he word for "humility" here is *tapeinophrosune*, from *tapeinos* meaning 'low lying'. I used to have a plaque in my office which read, "Be humble or you'll tumble." It was Solomon who wrote:

Pride goes before destruction,
and a haughty spirit before a fall.

Proverbs 16:18 (ESV)

Instead of haughtiness, we need the mindset of humility. Someone has described humility as "insight into one's own insignificance". It is the mindset of the person who is not conceited but who has a right attitude toward himself. It has been said:

True humility is not putting ourselves down but rather lifting up others.

The next verse demonstrates it. It shows it in action. It is called 'the two-four factor' (i.e. Philippians 2:4). Verse 4 says:

Let each of you look not only to his own interests, but also to the interests of others.

Philippians 2:4 (ESV)

This is a tough one because most of us secretly believe that we're better than those around us and that our music preference should be prescribed for everyone. 'To count others better' includes an idea borrowed from the mathematical world, and means, "Think about it and come to a conclusion." We are to count what is really there, add it up, and find out what is true. Are you looking out for the interests of others?

A young nurse once shared her story which beautifully illustrates Paul's point here. She said, "During my second month of nursing school, our professor gave us a pop quiz. I was a conscientious student and had breezed through the questions, until I read the last one: 'What is the first name of the woman who cleans the school?' Surely, this was some kind of joke. I had seen the cleaning woman several times. She was tall, dark-haired and in her 50s, but how would I know her name? I handed in my paper, leaving the last question blank. Before class ended, one student asked if the last question would count toward our quiz grade. 'Absolutely,' said the professor. 'In your careers you will meet many people. All are significant. They deserve your attention and care, even if all you do is smile and say hello.' I've never forgotten that lesson. I also learned her name was Dorothy."

Who is the 'Dorothy' in your life who needs your attention?

17

Norn Iron

Be prepared. You're up against far more than you can handle on your own. Take all the help you can get, every weapon God has issued, so that when it's all over but the shouting you'll still be on your feet. Truth, righteousness, peace, faith, and salvation are more than words. Learn how to apply them. You'll need them throughout your life.

Ephesians 6:13-16 (MSG)

Our guides tell us that there is no better way to get to know a country and its people than to mingle with the locals and engage in a bit of light-hearted banter. That applies here in Northern Ireland or "Norn Iron" as the locals call it. However, you might need a guide to speaking the local lingo. Let me help you with a few examples:

- Alright? – Hello.
- How's it cuttin'? – How are you?
- All the best! – Goodbye.
- On yer bike – Please leave.
- It's baltic – It's cold.
- It's roastin' – It's warm.
- A wee cup a tae in yer han – a cup of tea.
- Wee buns – easy.
- Poke – a whipped ice-cream.
- Is that you? – Are you ready?
- A wee dander – A leisurely walk.
- Keep 'er lit – Keep going.
- Footering – Wasting time.

That's just a taster. The community has coined these words and phrases which are completely alien to outsiders. Many Christian words and phrases can also be confusing to those who have not been raised in a Christian environment. Words such as 'atonement', 'discipleship', 'incarnation', 'grace', 'justification', 'sanctification', 'redemption' and 'righteousness' may seem foreign and unfamiliar to onlookers. We might wonder if such words have anything to do with our everyday, going-to-class, working, hanging-out-with-friends lives.

A grasp of some words is essential, as we see in today's verse. In other translations pieces of armour are attached to these words, such as "belt of truth", "breastplate of righteousness" and so on.[17] I used to focus so much on the armour that I failed to miss the key words such as "truth" and "righteousness".

Truth, righteousness, peace, faith and salvation. We need to understand the meaning of these core words and also how to accurately apply them to our daily living. Then we can stand firm.

---

[17] e.g. ESV

18

Shine Shoes Like a Soldier

Do not repay evil with evil or insult with insult. On the contrary, repay evil with blessing, because to this you were called so that you may inherit a blessing.

1 Peter 3:9 (NIV)

Do you polish your boots with military mirror-like precision? Do you notice other people's shoes? I've been told on more than one occasion that shoes agleam reflect an admirable character and are a hallmark of attention to the smallest detail. The older generation still take the view that you can 'tell a man by his shoes'. A scuffed shoe denoted a chap of chaotic behaviour, probably best avoided. A well-worn but highly polished brogue, on the other hand, suggested a man both professional and practical, able to take care of the things he loved. Our shoes speak volumes, especially if you have treated them to that one final triumphant buff with the chamois leather.

The following is a story which embedded in my memory many years ago. It's about a soldier who made it his practice to end every day with a devotional time of Bible-reading and prayer. As his fellow soldiers gathered in the barracks and retired for the night, he'd kneel by his bunk. His actions did not go unnoticed and it was not long before some of them began to mock and ridicule him. But one night the abuse went beyond words. As he bowed in prayer, one soldier threw his boots and hit him heavily smack in the face. The others jeered, looking for a fight, but there was no counterblow or retaliation. The next morning, when the boot-thrower woke up he couldn't believe what he saw. He was stunned. There at the foot of his bed were his boots – freshly polished and returned. Imagine shining the very boots that were thrown at you! That calls for a new level of grace.

It was Peter who told us:

Don't repay evil for evil. Don't retaliate with insults when people insult you. Instead, pay them back with a blessing. That is what God has called you to do, and he will grant you his blessing.

1 Peter 3:9 (NIV)

Paul phrased it this way:

Make sure that nobody pays back wrong for wrong, but always strive to do what is good for each other and for everyone else.

1 Thessalonians 5:15 (NIV)

Remember the example of Jesus who...

...while being reviled, He did not revile in return; while suffering, He uttered no threats, but kept entrusting Himself to Him who judges righteously.

1 Peter 2:23 (NASB)

Jesus prayed from the cross:

"Father, forgive them, for they do not know what they are doing."

Luke 23:34a (NIV)

The Roman soldiers had beaten and mocked him, and even as Jesus spoke these words they "divided up his clothes by casting lots"[18]. Yet Jesus understood that these people with their unresolved issues still needed salvation. A similar scenario took place in Acts 7, when Stephen was martyred. Like his Saviour before him, Stephen prayed, "Lay not this sin to their charge."[19]

It takes character, compassion and courage to act like the soldier in our story. As you go about your day, be a blessing to others and shine shoes like a soldier.

---

[18] Luke 23:34b (NIV)
[19] Acts 7:60 (KJV)

19

Anything Against Anyone

Bear with each other and forgive each other whatever grievances you may have against one another. Forgive as the Lord forgave you.

Colossians 3:13 (NIV)

A lecturer walked around a room while teaching his students. As he raised a glass of water, everyone expected they would be asked the usual 'half empty or half full' question. Instead, he inquired, "How much do you think this glass of water weighs?"

"Five hundred grams!" came a voice from the back.

"Six hundred!" said another student.

With the glass still in his outstretched hand, the professor continued, "What will happen if I hold it like this for a few minutes?"

"Nothing!" came the reply.

"Right, and if I hold it for an hour like this, what might happen?"

"Your hand will begin to hurt," said a student.

"Indeed. And what would happen if I held the glass in my hand like this for twenty-four hours?"

"You would be in tremendous pain," said one student.

"Your hand will probably go numb," said another.

"Your arm will be paralysed and we'll need to rush you to the hospital!" said a student on the last bench.

It is the same with nursing a grudge; the longer you carry it, the more it weighs you down. It can get so heavy, it stops you from living and paralyses your thinking. The reality of sharing this planet with others is that we will get hurt from time to time. That is why the Bible offers the advice in today's verse. Forgive each other whatever grievances you may have. Forgive as the Lord forgave you. God is challenging you to give up your personal grudges. Instead of nurturing an offence by rehearsing it repeatedly, instead of holding on to grudges and becoming bitter, frustrated individuals, God has called us to a higher standard: that of forgiveness. He invites you to break the cycle of bitterness that binds you to the wounds of yesterday. Jesus tells us:

> *"Whenever you stand praying, if you have anything against anyone, forgive him."*
>
> Mark 11:25 (AMP)

Anything against *anyone.* Be sure that when *you* pray, you no longer hold anything against anyone. We cannot experience the abundant life God has for us if we're carrying the weights of bitterness and unforgiveness around. They weigh us down, slow our steps, deplete our energy and steal our joy. It's time to let go and experience release. Ask God to search your heart.

> *Search me, God, and know my heart; test me and know my anxious thoughts. See if there is any offensive way in me, and lead me in the way everlasting.*
>
> Psalm 139:23-24 (NIV)

20

Welcome

Therefore welcome one another as Christ has welcomed you,
for the glory of God.

Romans 15:7 (ESV)

*H*ave you noticed how much we enjoy talking about food? We can bring home the bacon, work for peanuts, cut the mustard or have a finger in too many pies. We can butter someone up, egg someone on, cry over spilt milk, go bananas and upset the apple cart. We can be full of beans, one smart cookie, in a pickle or cheesed off. Or life can be a bowl of cherries and a piece of cake. You can take this with a pinch of salt. Maybe it's not your cup of tea.

You have probably heard the expression 'to give someone the cold shoulder'. The expression has long been believed to come from medieval times, when a welcome guest would be given shelter, drink and a lavish meal. Some guests might be less welcome or might start out welcome but take advantage of this cultural requirement for hospitality, and quite literally overstay their welcome. In such times, the host would serve a cold shoulder of mutton to the guest, probably leftovers, a meal usually reserved for household staff. It was a not-so-subtle way of saying, "Go away!"

Have you ever felt unwelcome? Have you ever had an experience where you were pretty sure people would rather you were not be around? Or, at least, they didn't seem too happy that you were there? I think all of us at some point in our life have. You could be standing in a room full of people but feeling very much alone. As Christians we should be welcoming. Hospitality and welcome streams throughout the Bible. Jesus told us:

"For if you love those who love you, what reward do you
have? Do not even the tax collectors do the same? And if you

greet only your brothers, what more are you doing than others? Do not even the Gentiles do the same?"

Matthew 5:46-48 (ESV)

Jesus' ministry was predicated upon accepting people. He erased the artificial boundaries of culture and status, looked beyond people's sin, and accepted them. He touched lepers, ate with sinners, visited the homes of tax collectors, and even washed the feet of the betrayer. Being a welcoming people is more than an abstract principle. It's more than words on paper. It's about real people and real lives.

He said to us:

"For I was hungry and you gave me food, I was thirsty and you gave me drink, I was a stranger and you welcomed me, I was naked and you clothed me, I was sick and you visited me, I was in prison and you came to me."

Matthew 25:35-36 (ESV)

The people said, "Lord, when was it that we saw you a stranger and welcomed you?" Jesus said, "Just as you did it to one of the least of these who are members of my family, you did it to me." Jesus says that when we welcome the stranger into the church, we are actually welcoming Him. "You welcomed Me." Christ has welcomed us with amazing love, mercy and kindness. Because of this, Paul says:

Therefore welcome one another as Christ has welcomed you, for the glory of God.

Romans 15:7 (ESV)

21

Our Ladybirds

Finally, be strong in the Lord and in the strength of his might.
Put on the whole armour of God, that you may be able to
stand against the schemes of the devil.

Ephesians 6:10-11 (ESV)

*T*he UK's favourite insect has been announced. In a poll that was answered by 7,500 eager entomologists, 40% claimed that the bee was certainly their favourite. The poll was set up in order to encourage people to appreciate the insects found in most gardens and voters had the choice of ten popular insects chosen by ecologists. Runner up in second place was the ladybird, with the Emperor Dragonfly and Small Tortoiseshell butterfly coming third and fourth. I must admit I love ladybirds. They are generally considered useful insects and one of the greatest allies of gardeners, who welcome ladybugs with open arms, knowing they will munch on the most prolific plant pests. They are nature's own 'pest' controllers and are more effective than poisonous chemicals.

The most common species of ladybird in Britain is the seven-spot ladybird. This bright red ladybird has seven spots and is thought to have inspired the name 'ladybird'. I'm told that in Europe, during the middle ages (long before the invention of chemical sprays that kill the pests), harmful insects were destroying the crops, so the farmers prayed to the Virgin Mary for help. Shortly after, the ladybirds came to the rescue and ate the plant-destroying insects and saved the crops. The European farmers gave thanks to Our Lady (the Virgin Mary) and named the beetle after her.

In early paintings Mary is seen wearing a red cloak just like the ladybird's colouration. In Germany, these insects go by the name *Marienkafer*, which means 'Mary beetles'. In America they are known as 'ladybugs' and scientists usually prefer the common name 'lady beetles'.

The bright colours of many ladybirds are to warn potential predators of their distastefulness (aposematism). Their colouring is likely a reminder to any animals that have tried to eat their kind before: "I taste awful." Insect-eating birds and other animals learn to avoid meals that come in red and black, and are more likely to steer clear of a ladybug lunch. A threatened ladybird may secrete the unappetising yellow substance, rich in toxic alkaloids, to protect itself.

The apostle Paul warns us to beware of Satan's devices and tactics.[20] How can we defend ourselves from his stealthy and deadly attacks? Paul wrote:

> *Be strong in the Lord and in his mighty power. Put on all of God's armor so that you will be able to stand firm against all strategies of the devil.*
>
> *Ephesians 6:10-11 (NLT)*

This is a comprehensive defence strategy, and we have to pay attention to all parts of this protective armour God offers. If we do, we will be able to withstand Satan's attacks. Don't forget, you are more than a conqueror through Jesus Christ.

---

[20] See 2 Corinthians 2:11

22

Have a Shower

For I have satiated the weary soul, and every languishing soul have I replenished.

Jeremiah 31:25 (Darby Bible)

*T*he great debate rages on: baths versus showers. Google it and you will see what I mean. Which do you prefer? Some promote baths as a great means of relaxation and soaking your tired muscles. Others see it solely as sitting in a vat of one's own dirt and watching your fingers become prune-like. I was wandering along the aisle in the supermarket which stocks showers gels and I must admit their titles seemed most inviting. Here's a selection:

- feel revived with mandarin and lemongrass;
- feel uplifted with pink grapefruit and basil;
- feel invigorated with lemon and rosemary;
- feel energised with keylime and peppermint;
- feel refreshed with eucalyptus and citrus oils;
- feel active with lemongrass and sea salt;
- feel relaxed with lavender and water lily;
- feel rejuvenated with orange oil and vitamin E;
- feel calm with chamomile and jojoba oil.

Don't we all desire to feel revived, uplifted, invigorated, energised, refreshed etc.? God desires it for you too. He wants you to feel replenished today. Weariness – whether physical, emotional or spiritual – comes to us all. Isaiah reminds us that although we become tired, the Lord, the everlasting God, the Creator of the ends of the earth "will not grow tired or weary"[21]. How easily we forget that in every situation "[the

---

[21] Isaiah 40:28 (NIV)

Lord] gives strength to the weary and increases the power of the weak"
[22] The Psalmist declared:

O God, you cause abundant showers to fall on your chosen people.

When they are tired, you sustain them...

Psalm 68:9 (NET)

Allow God to shower you today with His abundance, with "showers of blessing"[23]. The word "shower" in the Hebrew is *geshem*, which means 'to pour down in a heavy shower'. God wants to rain blessings in your life – and not just a light rain of blessings. He wants to pour down *heavy* showers of blessings on you! Allow Him to uplift you and revive you. Open His Word and receive it because...

The law of the Lord is perfect, reviving the soul...

Psalm 19:7 (ESV)

---

[22] Isaiah 40:29 (NIV)
[23] Ezekiel 34:26 (NLT)

23

A Penny for Your Thoughts

Finally, brothers and sisters, whatever is true, whatever is noble, whatever is right, whatever is pure, whatever is lovely, whatever is admirable – if anything is excellent or praiseworthy – think about such things.

Philippians 4:8 (NIV)

"A penny for your thoughts" is said when you want to know what another person is thinking, usually because they have been quiet for a while. The earliest record of the expression in print is by Sir Thomas More in his book *Four Last Things,* published in 1522. The expression became so well used that it was often shortened to "a penny for them" or even just "penny". Some people wonder if it might be insulting, since a penny is worth next to nothing today, and might produce the sharp response, "Is that all you think my thoughts are worth?" That certainly wasn't the idea behind it, since a penny was worth a sizeable sum when the phrase was first written down.

Your thoughts are valuable to God. The Scripture reminds us that as we think, so we are.[24] The mind and our thoughts are a major topic in Scripture. God actually tells us what to think about in today's verse.

The verse gives us eight questions to ask about our thought life.

Is it true? Truth is the first test.

Is it noble? The word refers to that which is worthy of respect and awe-inspiring.

Is it right? This means in conformity to God's standards.

Is it pure? The word means 'free from defilement, stainless, that which will not contaminated, clean, holy'.

Is it lovely? This word is used only here in the New Testament. It literally means 'love towards' and thus gracious.

---

[24] See Proverbs 23:7

Is it admirable? That is, is it laudable and worthy of contemplation, or is it negative and critical?

Is it excellent? Excellent refers to moral goodness and those things that God himself would approve.

Is it praiseworthy? A good way to counter critical thoughts is to dwell on praiseworthy thoughts.

We are even commanded to bring every thought into captivity of Christ:

> *We destroy arguments and every lofty opinion raised against the knowledge of God, and take every thought captive to obey Christ. (ESV)*
>
> *2 Corinthians 10:5*

Your thoughts are worth much more than a penny. They are determinative of how you will live your life.

24

Go the Extra Mile

If a soldier demands that you carry his gear for a mile, carry it two miles.

Matthew 5:41 (NLT)

*M*any common English phrases find their origins in Scripture. Here are a few which have found their way into our modern vernacular:

- "By the skin of your teeth" from Job 19:20;
- "Can a leopard change his spots?" from Jeremiah 13:23;
- "Drop in a bucket" from Isaiah 40:15;
- "Wash your hands of the matter" from Matthew 27:24;
- "Wits' end" from Psalm 107:27;
- "A law unto themselves" from Romans 2:14;
- "A sign of the times" from Matthew 16:3; and
- "Go the extra mile" from Matthew 5:41.

"Going the extra mile" is a popular phrase that stems from the teaching of Jesus in today's reading. Its roots are found all the way back in first-century Palestine. One of the marvels of Roman conquest was a vast system of highways. There were more than fifty thousand miles of these Roman roads throughout the Empire. The Roman mile was a thousand paces, or 1,520 yards. At each single mile there was a stone marker. Back in Jesus' day, Roman soldiers could lawfully commandeer able-bodied civilians to carry their gear (which could weigh upwards of a hundred pounds) for one mile without any compensation. It was unfair, inconvenient and often backbreaking. But Jesus encouraged His followers to respond in a new and unexpected way, one that would reflect the generous love of God's kingdom instead of unlawful resistance. Can you imagine the bombshell this must have been as it fell upon the ears of those under Roman occupation who were listening to His sermon? Jesus called upon His hearers to do what was required of them — and then some.

There is the obligated mile motived by law. Then there is the 'over and above' mile motivated by love.

Imagine a first-century boy working at his trade. A Roman soldier calls to him and demands that he carry his backpack for one mile down the road. This command interrupts the lad's whole day and takes him away from his work. But he has no choice. However, this boy is a second miler. They approach the one-mile marker and instead of putting down the pack and marching back home, he volunteers to go an extra mile with the soldier.

That extra mile will make a difference in your relationships at work or at school, or in your home. Someone who journeys on the extra mile has a way of lightening the load of those around them. Paul said:

Bear ye one another's burdens, and so fulfil the law of Christ.

Galatians 6:2 (KJV)

Why should each Christian go the extra mile? Because the Lord Jesus Christ went all the way to Calvary for us. It took Him to the cross where He bore the weight, not of a Roman soldier's backpack, but of our own sin. Today perhaps God will use your extra-mile efforts to help others see what His outrageous love is all about. Go beyond what is required. Do more than expected. Allow Christ's love to compel you.[25]

---

[25] See 2 Corinthians 5:14

25

Allow Your Soul to Sing

O Sovereign LORD! You made the heavens and earth by your strong hand and powerful arm. Nothing is too hard for you!
Jeremiah 32:17 (NLT)

*I*n 2013, *Songs of Praise* conducted a nationwide survey in the UK. Tens of thousands of people voted for their favourite hymn. The hymns which ranked in the top ten were:

1. How Great Thou Art;
2. In Christ Alone;
3. Be Still, For The Presence Of The Lord;
4. Dear Lord And Father Of Mankind;
5. Here I Am, Lord;
6. And Can It Be;
7. Abide With Me;
8. Guide Me, O Thou Great Jehovah;
9. Make Me A Channel Of Your Peace;
10. The Day Thou Gavest Lord Is Ended.

How Great Thou Art has its origins as a poem in a small town in Sweden. It was written by a sailor-turned-lay-minister by the name of Carl Boberg (1859-1940). Boberg tells us how it came about:

It was in 1885, and in the time of year when everything seemed to be in its richest colouring; the birds were singing in trees and wherever they could find a perch. On a particular afternoon, some friends and I had been to Kronobäck where we had participated in an afternoon service. As we were returning a thunderstorm began to appear on the horizon. We hurried to shelter. There were loud claps of thunder, and the lighting flashed across the sky. Strong winds swept over the meadows and billowing fields of grain. However, the storm was soon over and the clear sky appeared with a beautiful rainbow... After reaching my home, I opened my window toward the sea. The church bells were playing the tune of a hymn. That same evening, I wrote a poem which I titled, 'O Store Gud,' (How Great Thou Art).

Boberg would never know the influence of his poem. He died in 1940, over a decade before *How Great Thou Art* began its orbit around the world by way of the Billy Graham New York City Crusade where it was sung ninety-nine times.

I love the references in it to creation, to salvation and especially to the coming of Christ. You cannot sing this majestic hymn of praise and adoration without realising anew the omnipotence of the Creator who did it all. The song has become synonymous with trusting in the Divine power of God.

This reminds me of today's passage. God merely spoke the universe into being, a universe that astronomers estimate contains more than a hundred billion galaxies. But all the power contained in this entire universe is but a small representation of the unlimited power of God. No task is too big for Him. Nothing is too hard for Him. No need is too great for Him to meet. No problem is too complicated for Him to solve. No foe is too strong for Him to conquer. No prayer is too difficult for Him to answer. He longs to exhibit His power in our lives.

Yours, O LORD, is the greatness and the power and the glory and the victory and the majesty, for all that is in the heavens and in the earth is yours. Yours is the kingdom, O LORD, and you are exalted as head above all.

1 Chronicles 29:11 (ESV)

Take time today to behold the wonder of God's creation and the evidence of His power and be amazed at the awesomeness of God. Allow your soul to sing. As the refrain says,

Then sings my soul
My Saviour, God, to Thee,
How great thou art,
How great thou art.

26

A Torch, a Jar and a Trumpet

And he divided the 300 men into three companies and put trumpets into the hands of all of them and empty jars, with torches inside the jars.

Judges 7:16 (ESV)

Gideon had to watch as God whittled the army of Israel from thirty-two thousand down to only three hundred. Firstly, those who were trembling with fear were asked to turn back and leave the scene of battle. Interestingly twenty-two thousand men left. Then God asked Gideon to take the ten thousand men who remained to the water. God said:

"Separate those who lap the water with their tongues as a dog laps from those who kneel down to drink."

Judges 7:5 (NIV)

Only three hundred men who lapped with their hands to their mouths were selected.

In Judges 7:8, we find that Gideon and his group of three hundred men are about to engage the enemy – the Midianites. Three hundred against 135,000! Impossible odds from man's perspective. Gideon and his men were outnumbered by their enemies, but they followed God's directions. The war strategy was very interesting. These three hundred men were handed trumpets and empty jars with torches inside. They would carry only three things: a torch, a jar and a trumpet. Can you imagine Gideon as he was gathering his army of three hundred around him saying, "It's time to go into battle. Here are your weapons. Here's your trumpet! Here's your clay jar. And here's your torch." We may not fully understand His plans, but we can fully trust His promises; and it's faith in Him that gives the victory.

Interestingly, breaking pottery spooks camels. Trumpets were usually blown only by captains, not ordinary soldiers, so Gideon makes it sound as if he has an army of three hundred thousand. In the world of ancient warfare, a commander with a number of troops under him would sound a trumpet to call his men into battle. So when Gideon and each one of his men blew a trumpet, the Midianites thought that each of the three hundred men was a commander of many others, and that a huge army had surrounded them.

Earlier in the night, Gideon had overheard a Midianite soldier interpret his compatriot's dream to mean that God would employ the "sword of Gideon"[26] to defeat the Midianites. Presumably, word of the dream had spread in the camp. Therefore, the cry, "A sword for the Lord and for Gideon!" inspired fear in the Midianite camp. Waking rapidly, with all that light and noise, would have been terribly disorienting. Without benefit of daylight, the Midianite soldiers, believing themselves to be under attack, turned their swords against what they assumed to be an onrushing army. In so doing, they unwittingly cut each other down. The victory came, not through conventional weapons, but through God's ways.

> *Some trust in chariots, and some in horses;*
> *But we will remember the name of the LORD of God.*
>
> *Psalm 20:7 (NKJV)*

That's the key.

> *The Lord is my Light and my Salvation – whom shall I fear or dread? The Lord is the Refuge and Stronghold of my life – of whom shall I be afraid? When the wicked, even my enemies and my foes, came upon me to eat up my flesh, they stumbled and fell. Though a host encamp against me, my heart shall not fear; though war arise against me, [even then] in this will I be confident.*
>
> *Psalm 27:1 (AMPC)*

God loves to use ordinary, weak human vessels to do extraordinary things. God loves to use our weakness to show His strength. So let our lives be as trumpets boldly announcing our testimony and declaring who we are in Christ, more than conquerors in Him. Let our lives be as broken

---

[26] Judges 7:14 (ESV)

clay pots[27] which allow the light of Christ to shine from us. Let boldness, brokenness and brightness define us.

---

[27] earthen vessels; see 2 Corinthians 4:10-11

27

Painting by Numbers

I will instruct you and teach you in the way you should go; I will counsel you with my eye upon you.

Psalm 32:8

*P*ainting by numbers is a system whereby a picture is divided into shapes, each marked with a number that corresponds to a particular colour. The kit will include a brush, little pots of paint in however many colours you'll need, and a printed outline of the picture. The idea is that you paint in each shape and ultimately the picture emerges as a finished painting. Leonardo himself invented a form of it, assigning assistants to paint areas on a work that he had already sketched out and numbered. The key to the kit, however, is to follow instructions. That was my downfall. Apparently, each kit comes with its own instruction manual, "How to Paint by the Numbers." Advice is given such as:

- "Paint one colour at a time, from the largest areas of this colour to the smallest."
- "Working from the top of the painting down helps prevent accidentally disturbing wet paint." Oops! I should have read that!
- "Keep a jar of clean water for washing your brush to hand, as well as a cloth for wiping and drying the brush."
- "Don't dunk the brush into the paint all the way up to the ferrule, just the tip." Oops! That would have been a useful instruction to follow.
- "Be meticulous about cleaning the brush before dipping it into another colour. You don't want to contaminate a colour..." No, you don't!

Now I know that following instructions is for my benefit. The Bible has been described as God's instruction manual for life. The handy mnemonic device for B.I.B.L.E. is Basic Instructions Before Leaving Earth. The Bible makes us wise for salvation and is profitable for instruction in righteousness, as Paul declares in 2 Timothy 3:16-17. The Bible gives us full and complete instruction in how to live our life here on the earth in preparation for an eternal life with the Father in heaven.

Ignoring God's instructions for our lives will lead to some very frustrating steps. We will enjoy life more when we purpose to live our lives in accordance with our Maker's instructions. God says to each one of us, "I will instruct you and teach you in the way you should go." Proverbs 3 advises us:

> *Do not forget my teaching, but let your heart keep my commandments; for length of days and years of life [worth living] and tranquility and prosperity [the wholeness of life's blessings] they will add to you.*
>
> *Proverbs 3:1-2 (AMP)*

God offers instruction but we must accept it and apply it to our lives. As Charles R. Swindoll phrased it:

> *Application is the essential link between God's instruction and change in our lives.*

Can you say with the Psalmist:

> *Your commands are always with me and make me wiser than my enemies. I have more insight than all my teachers, for I meditate on your statutes. I have more understanding than the elders, for I obey your precepts.*
>
> *Psalm 119:98-100 (NIV)*

28

The Urgency of the Hour

We must work the works of Him who sent Me as long as it is day; night is coming when no one can work.

John 9:4

*I*n the UK the clocks go forward one hour at 1am on the last Sunday in March, and back one hour at 2am on the last Sunday in October. The period when the clocks are one hour ahead is called British Summer Time (BST). To avoid confusion, many use the phrase "spring forward – fall back" to remember when the clocks change. Why do we do this? Daylight Saving Time (or 'Summer Time', as it's known in many parts of the world) was created to make better use of the long sunlight hours of the summer. By 'springing' clocks forward an hour in March, we move an hour of daylight from the morning to the evening. Of course, this reverses when they go back, meaning it gets dark earlier in the afternoon.

Jesus spoke the words in today's reader. He stated that He had a particular work to do on earth, but He used the pronoun "we" because we are part of that work! 2 Corinthians 5:18,20 shows us our part.

Christ reconciled us to himself and gave us the ministry of reconciliation; ... Therefore, we are ambassadors for Christ, God making his appeal through us.

2 Corinthians 5:18,20 (ESV)

Paul previously grasped this fact in Acts 20:

"But my life is worth nothing to me unless I use it for finishing the work assigned me by the Lord Jesus – the work of telling others the Good News about the wonderful grace of God."

Acts 20:24 (NLT)

Jesus understood God's plan for His life to be a 'must' ("We must work..."), not an option. At the age of twelve, He said:

I must be about my Father's business.

Luke 2:49 (KJV)

He also understood the urgency of the hour. The need was urgent. Urgency is that strong prompting that makes us do something now! We have an allotted season to work – time is short. God has a designated time frame "while it is day"[28].

There are many of us who are always so swept up in our daily chores, and the business and busyness of life, that we forget that we are running out of time to reach the lost. It is like we are waiting for something to happen such as another revival. But Jesus says that we need to look at the fields because they are white already to harvest. Today is the day of salvation.

May we always abound in the work of the Lord[29] and adopt as our personal motto the words spoken by our Lord: "We must work the works of Him who sent Me as long as it is day; night is coming when no one can work." As we meditate on this verse, may we realise afresh the urgency of the hour.

---

[28] John 9:4 (KJV)
[29] See 1 Corinthians 15:58

29

What do You Call the Dot on an 'i'?

"For assuredly, I say to you, till heaven and earth pass away, one jot or one tittle will by no means pass from the law till all is fulfilled."

Matthew 5:18 (NKJV)

*J*ots and tittles have to do with letters and pen strokes in Hebrew writing. A jot referred to the smallest letter of the alphabet and a tittle was even smaller than a jot. A tittle was a letter extension, a pen stroke which differentiated one Hebrew letter from another. The dot on top of our letter 'i' is called a tittle. 'Tittle' sounds appropriately like the words 'tiny' and 'little' merged together. An expression associated with 'tittle' is 'to a T', being a shortened form of 'to a tittle', meaning 'precise, down to the very last detail'. The jot is still used by us when making a brief note; we jot it down.

Jesus uses the words in today's verse from the Sermon on the Mount. In the previous verse He said:

"Do not think that I have come to abolish the Law or the Prophets; I have not come to abolish them but to fulfil them."

Matthew 5:17 (ESV)

What was written in Hebrew Scripture must be fulfilled and it is amazing to see how Jesus fulfilled the Old Testament prophetic words.

When He was walking along the road to Emmaus, He spoke to the disciples and we are told:

...beginning at Moses and all the Prophets, He expounded to them in all the Scriptures the things concerning Himself.

Luke 24:27 (NKJV)

What a sermon this must have been. No wonder their hearts burned within them. The law and the prophets had all borne testimony, either directly or indirectly, to Christ. In John 1 we are told that Philip found Nathaniel and told him:

"We have found the One Moses wrote about in the Law (and so did the prophets): Jesus the son of Joseph, from Nazareth!"

John 1:45 (HCSB)

How deficient our Biblical knowledge would be, specifically concerning Jesus, if we steered clear of the Old Testament. When Christ commenced His public ministry in the synagogue at Nazareth with the words of Isaiah, "The Spirit of the Lord is upon me, because he hath anointed me to preach the gospel to the poor,"[30] He said:

This day is this Scripture fulfilled in your ears.

Luke 4:21 (KJV)

As He drew near to the Cross, our Saviour said:

Behold we go up to Jerusalem, and all things that are written by the prophets concerning the Son of Man shall be accomplished.

Luke 18:31 (KJV)

Jesus said:

"'Man shall not live by bread alone, but by every word that proceeds from the mouth of God.'"

Matthew 4:4 (NKJV)

Let's value every word, remembering that even the jot and tittle matter to God.

All Scripture is given by inspiration of God, and is profitable for doctrine, for reproof, for correction, for instruction in righteousness, that the man of God may be complete, thoroughly equipped for every good work.

2 Timothy 3:16-17 (KJV)

---

[30] Luke 4:18 (KJV)

30

Collective Nouns

And believers were increasingly added to the Lord, multitudes of both men and women.

Acts 5:14

Do you remember English class and learning about collective nouns? Collective nouns are names for a collection or a number of people or things. For example, a group of rhinos is called a crash; a group of kangaroos is called a mob; a group of whales is called a pod; a group of owls is called a parliament; a group of camels is called a caravan; a group of starlings is called a murmuration. We also talk of a pandemonium of parrots, a bloat of hippos, a business of ferrets, a congress of baboons, a conspiracy of lemurs.

A collective term for referring to Christians in the book of Acts is the word "believers". For example:

All the believers were together and had everything in common.

Acts 2:44 (NIV)

All the believers were one in heart and mind.

Acts 4:32 (NIV)

And believers were increasingly added to the Lord, multitudes of both men and women.

Acts 5:14 (NKJV)

In his Gospel John told us his reason for writing. He said:

But these are written so that you may believe that Jesus is the Christ, the Son of God, and that by believing you may have life in his name.

John 20:31 (ESV)

Do you believe Jesus Christ is who the Bible says He is, and are you trusting Him as your Saviour?

Jesus promises:

"Most assuredly, I say to you, he who believes in Me, the works that I do he will do also; and greater works than these he will do, because I go to My Father."

John 14:12 (NKJV)

"Truly I say to you, whoever says to this mountain, 'Be taken up and cast into the sea,' and does not doubt in his heart, but believes that what he says is going to happen, it shall be granted him."

Mark 11:23 (NASB)

"He who believes in Me, as the Scripture has said, out of his heart will flow rivers of living water."

John 7:38 (NKJV)

Are you a 'he/she who believes'? Can you say with Paul:

I am not ashamed: for I know whom I have believed, and am persuaded that he is able to keep that which I have committed unto him against that day.

2 Timothy 1:12 (KJV)

" *Whom*," Paul says. Quite another thing from "what". "I know *what* I have believed" – that is good. "I know *whom* I have believed" – that is the essence of faith. Paul's faith is about the relationship he has with Christ. "I know ... and I am persuaded" leaves no room for doubt. His belief affected his behaviour on a daily basis. It wasn't just a creed; it was a commitment to live each day in the way which reflected God's image and interests. Faith must make a difference to how we live. As Brennan Manning said:

The greatest cause of atheism is Christians who acknowledge Jesus with their lips, then walk out the door and deny him with their lifestyle. That is what an unbelieving world simply finds unbelievable.

Let us live out our faith today knowing whom we have believed and doing His works, seeing the mountains move and the rivers of living water flow from within us. May our faithfulness be the result of our faith;

may our witness be winsome and may we see believers "increasingly added to the Lord, multitudes of both men and women"[31].

---

[31] Acts 5:14 (NKJV)

June

July

July

1

Spot the Difference

...tell others of the night-and-day difference he made for you
– from nothing to something, from rejected to accepted.

1 Peter 2:9-10 (MSG)

*M*ost people loved playing spot the difference as children, and some still do even as adults. Apparently, it is an excellent game for the brain and your cognitive development. You are given two pictures which are very similar, but there are a few subtle differences in the pictures. How many differences can you spot? How observant are you? I'm still tempted to play online, especially when the challenge pops us, "Only a genius can find them: Can YOU spot the differences in this photo?"

1 Peter tells us that we are "God's instruments to do his work and speak out for Him, to tell others of the night-and-day difference he made for you – from nothing to something, from rejected to accepted." The night-and-day difference. From nothing to something, from rejected to accepted. He goes on to say:

Once you were not a people, but now you are God's people;
once you had not received mercy, but now you have received
mercy.

1 Peter 2:10 (ESV)

Once you were... Now you are...

In Colossians 3 we spot the differences because Paul contrasts the "once you were" way of life with the "now you are" way of life. The same happens in Ephesians 2. We were dead in our sins. We were separated from God. We were "children of wrath"[32] – deserving of God's punishment. We walked according to the course of this world. It's a

---

[32] Ephesians 2:3 (ESV)

pitiful picture but then we read in Ephesians 2:4[33], "But God." Now the picture is different. We are alive in Christ and reconciled to God. We are His glorious masterpiece[34] and the recipients of the "exceeding riches of His grace [and] His kindness" [35].

Take time today to thank for the night-and-day difference He has made to your life.

---

[33] AMP
[34] See Ephesians 2:10
[35] Ephesians 2:7 (NKJV)

2

Big Fat Lies

If we say we have no sin, we deceive ourselves, and the truth is not in us. If we confess our sins, He is faithful and just to forgive us our sins and to cleanse us from all unrighteousness. If we say we have not sinned, we make Him a liar, and His word is not in us.

1 John 1:8-10 (NKJV)

Low-Carb Diets. The Paleo Diet. The Atkins Diet. The Mediterranean Diet. Serial dieters may try them all in an effort to shed excess weight. I read recently that there is a new diet that is all the rage. You can eat all you see of everything you don't like. I'm not sure it will take off.

One of the most common pieces of dieting advice is to eat "everything in moderation". But many people have a skewed sense of what 'moderation' means. According to a new British study, we under-report the number of calories we eat each day. That's right. We are all lying – both to ourselves and to others – about how much we eat… by quite a lot. Researchers found that we underestimate how many calories we're eating by 30% to 50%. That means we're chowing down on an extra thousand calories per person, per day – on top on the average of two thousand.

Here are some of the lies we tell ourselves:

- "I'll burn it all off in the gym."
- "I'll keep it light by ordering a diet Coke with my double cheese Big Mac and extra large fries."
- "Biscuit pieces and crumbs contain no calories; the process of breaking causes calorie leakage."
- "Things licked off spoons have no calories, especially whipped cream."
- "A balanced diet is a burger in both hands."

- "Chocolate chips are fattening. So are chocolate chip cookies! However, chocolate chips eaten while making chocolate chip cookies have no calories whatsoever."
- "If no one saw you polish off half the packet of triple chocolate digestives, it didn't really happen."
- "If you eat something and no-one sees you eating it, it has no calories."
- "Food used for medicinal purposes never counts, e.g. barley sugar sweets, hot chocolate, cough syrup."

The Bible tells us that we can deceive ourselves in other ways, as in today's reading. If we say we have no sin, we deceive ourselves, and the truth is not in us. Beware of self-deception. Self-deception is our ability to justify things we know are not right. It can cause a local church to think they are great when actually God sees them as wretched, poor and blind.[36] Stop excusing. Stop tolerating. We can come up with many pretexts to justify our actions, but if they don't tally with the precepts of God's Word they are simply ways we deceive ourselves. What self-destructive behaviour in your life are you pretending isn't there? What activity or attitude is unhealthy? What are the lies you are telling yourself that keep you from making lasting changes in your life? It's time to admit and quit.

---

[36] See Revelation 3:14-22

3

The Heart of Obedience

I have been crucified with Christ. It is no longer I who live, but Christ who lives in me. And the life I now live in the flesh I live by faith in the Son of God, who loved me and gave himself for me.

Galatians 2:20 (ESV)

The middle three letters of the word obedience are 'die'. They are very significant. The world's philosophy says, live for self; but God's Word says, die to self. Dying to self expresses the true essence of obedience in which we take up our cross and follow Christ. Thus Paul said, "I have been crucified with Christ; it is no longer I who live, but Christ lives in me."

I remember seeing an illustration on a whiteboard where the letter "I" from this verse was written in bold in the centre. With just a small stroke of the pen the "I" was transformed into a cross which became the centre focus.

The Greek word for obedience is *hupakouo*. It is a compound word that means literally 'to listen under'. It carried with it the thought of submission. We die to self and submit ourselves to His way of doing things. Jesus said:

"If anyone would come after me, let him deny himself and take up his cross daily and follow me."

Luke 9:23 (ESV)

Following is obedience.

The story is told that when Augustine was still without God and without hope, Paul's words in Romans 13:14 brought conviction:

But put ye on the Lord Jesus Christ, and make not provision for the flesh, to fulfil its lusts.

Romans 13:14 (KJV)

Augustine acknowledged his sinfulness, accepted Jesus as his Saviour, and became a different person. His entire outlook on life began to change because of his new nature. One day he had to return to his old haunts in Rome. As he walked along, a promiscuous woman whose company he had formerly enjoyed began calling, "Augustine, Augustine, it is I!" He took one look and shuddered. Augustine took flight with the woman in pursuit of him crying out the same words, "Augustine, it is I." The story concludes with Augustine shouting back to her, "It is you, but it is not I." He had found the secret of Paul's words, "I live; yet not I, but Christ liveth in me."[37]

George Müller,[38] when questioned about his spirituality, responded simply, "One day George Müller died." He said, "There was a day when I died, utterly died – died to George Müller, his opinions, preferences, tastes, and will; died to the world, its approval or censure; died to the approval or blame even of my brethren and friends – and since then I have only to show myself approved to God."

Have we truly understood the heart of obedience?

---

[37] Galatians 2:20 (KJV)
[38] George Muller (1805-1898)

4

The Snowball Effect

For when I kept silent, my bones wasted away
  through my groaning all day long.
For day and night your hand was heavy upon me;
  my strength was dried up as by the heat of summer. Selah.
I acknowledged my sin to you,
  and I did not cover my iniquity;
I said, "I will confess my transgressions to the LORD,"
  and you forgave the iniquity of my sin. Selah.

Psalm 32:3-5 (ESV)

I shall start by introducing a term that many of you are probably familiar with: 'the snowball effect'. It is a figurative term for a process that starts from an initial state of small significance and builds on itself, becoming larger with each passing moment. The term comes from the practice of making a small snowball at the top of a large hill and rolling it down the snow-covered hillside. The original small snowball grows with tremendous rapidity. The more surface area it covers, the more mass it obtains, and vice versa. That is to say, it gets very big, very fast. Such is the phenomenon of the snowball effect.

I decided that it would be an excellent idea to put this snowball theory into practice. The setting at the back of our home was perfect for the execution of the plan, and immediately team Gregg began to set it into action. A small ball was selected and then set in motion down the gently sloping hill. The mass of snow lumbered down the hill and began to grow larger. In the course of its travel, however, it picked up dirt, twigs, pine needles and unwanted elements, becoming increasingly hard and icy. Very soon the snowball veered out of control and crashed.

Sin can be like a snowball – starting small enough with a simple thought, but when we act on the thought the ball starts rolling. Soon it gains mass and momentum. The snowball effect of sin, its consequences and its ongoing effects are mentioned hundreds of times in the Bible, a prime example being that of King David. One night, David was walking around on his roof and saw a beautiful woman named Bathsheba taking a bath. Her beauty tempted David, and instead of turning away from that temptation, he inquired about her. He had Bathsheba brought to his palace, and we know the story. She sent word back to David that she was pregnant, so David tried to think of a way to hide his sin. First, he sent word to Joab to send Bathsheba's husband, Uriah, back from the war. David was hoping that Uriah would go home and sleep with his wife so her pregnancy could be attributed to him, but Uriah refused to go home while his friends were still fighting a battle. Since Uriah would not cooperate with David's plan, David told Joab to put Uriah at the front line of the war so that he would be killed in battle. He was trying to justify and further hide his actions, to cloak them in the guise of "stuff happens during times of war". But every sin that goes uncorrected gives birth to a greater life of sin; everything snowballed and spiralled out of control. Thankfully, today's verse in Psalm 32 tells us that David acknowledged his sin.

David sought and received God's forgiveness. The Hebrew word for 'forgiven' literally means 'lifted off'. The weight of sin had taken its toll on David's life but we read the key words "acknowledge", "not cover" and "confess". His confession was like opening the floodgates of a dam and he pens Psalm 32 telling us:

> Blessed is the one whose transgression is forgiven.
>
> *Psalm 32:1 (ESV)*

Let's beware of the snowball effect of sin and remember those key words today: "acknowledge", "not cover" and "confess".

5

Please Look After This Bear. Thank You.

Treat everyone you meet with dignity.

1 Peter 2:17 (MSG)

A duffle coat, a hard stare, marmalade sandwiches, darkest Peru. You have guessed the connection. Michael Bond's marmalade-sandwich-loving Peruvian bear first sauntered onto the page in 1958's *A Bear Called Paddington.* Paddington's address – 32 Windsor Gardens in Notting Hill – does not exist in real life. Author Michael Bond amalgamated his parents' address at Winser Drive, Reading, with his own in Arundel Gardens. Tourists who descend upon the real-life Windsor Gardens in west London are often disappointed to find a street of council flats and no number 32.

Before his fictional version appeared on page, Paddington existed as a real teddy bear. Bond saw it "left on a shelf in a London shop and felt sorry for it" on Christmas Eve 1956, and took it home as a present for his wife Brenda. The couple were living near Paddington Station at the time, so Bond named the bear Paddington and started to write stories about it.

Michael Bond says that the inspiration for Paddington came from seeing Jewish evacuee children pass through Reading Station from London during the Kindertransport of the late 30s. They all had a label round their neck, he says, with their name and address on and a little case or package containing all their treasured possessions. And so Paddington, in his blue duffle coat and red hat, has a sign round his neck from his relatives back in darkest Peru with a simple request: "Please look after this bear. Thank you." Why is Paddington so popular? Nestled deep in our hearts is the longing for a home full of love, understanding and stability. We all wear an invisible label that says, "Please look after this bear. Thank you." We were created with love, to give love and receive love. The Bible insistently tells us to love others, accept them, treat them fairly and honourably. However, we are all too quick to put a label on people. Don't label people; love them.

Jesus did not categorise, stereotype or slap a label on those He encountered. He loved them and treated each one with dignity: the woman at the well, the woman taken in adultery, Nicodemus, even Judas and Peter. We are to do the same. Peter tells us, "Treat everyone you meet with dignity." *Everyone.* How do we do that? We remember that all are made in the image of God, His creation. Showing honour and respect doesn't mean we embrace or endorse what they do or even what they believe, but we respect the individual as a creation of God. God isn't finished with any of us, is He? Let's not forget the grace we have been shown.

We cannot love others like Christ... without Christ.

We love each other because he loved us first.

1 John 4:19 (NLT)

So represent Him well today treating everyone you meet with dignity. See them only with the label, "Please look after this person. Thank you."

6

Not One Word Has Failed

...imitate those who through faith and patience inherit the promises.

Hebrews 6:12 (NKJV)

*I*n my brain teaser book I came across this one:

Q: Before Mount Everest was discovered, what was the highest mountain on earth? A: Still Mount Everest; it just hadn't been discovered yet, but it had always been there.

It reminded me of God's promises. Thousands of promises of God's miraculous favour, equipping, help and provision are in the Word of God and are ready to be discovered and released into your life! It's time for us to tap into God's limitless supply and live in the reality of all that God desires. The way some people use the term, a promise is nothing more than a good intention easily discarded. Like the proverbial rule, promises are made to be broken. But when God makes a promise, it's backed with more than just good intentions and wishful thinking. He is giving us His absolutely trustworthy word. None of God's promises in the Bible ever fail. It's in the Bible:

...not one word has failed of all the good things that the LORD your God promised concerning you. All have come to pass for you; not one of them has failed.

Joshua 23:14 (ESV)

God invites us to...

...imitate those who through faith and patience inherit the promises.

Hebrews 6:12 (NKJV)

Notice that faith and patience are necessary to inherit the promises. Hebrews 11 gives us a compilation of characters who stepped out in faith and obtained the promises of God. It says:

...who through faith conquered kingdoms, enforced justice, obtained promises, stopped the mouths of lions.

Hebrews 11:33 (ESV)

One such character listed in this chapter is Abraham. In Romans 4:19-21 we learn about Abraham and how he inherited God's promises.

And being not weak in faith, he considered not his own body now dead, when he was about an hundred years old, neither yet the deadness of Sarah's womb: he staggered not at the promise of God through unbelief; but was strong in faith, giving glory to God; and being fully persuaded that, what he had promised, he was able also to perform.

Romans 4:19-21 (KJV)

God promises us that we will not lack anything that is needed.

Oh, fear the LORD, you His saints!
There is no want to those who fear Him.
The young lions lack and suffer hunger;
But those who seek the LORD shall not lack any good thing.

Psalm 34:9-10 (NKJV)

He promises that when we call on Him, He will answer.

He shall call upon Me, and I will answer him,
I will be with him in trouble;
I will deliver him and honor him.

Psalm 91:15 (NKJV)

He promises to go with us.

Be strong and of a good courage, fear not nor be afraid of them; for the LORD thy God, He it is that doth go with thee, He will not fail thee nor forsake thee.

Deuteronomy 31:6 (KJV)

He promises to help us at every stage of life.

And even to your old age I am He; and even to hoar hairs will I carry you: I have made, and I will bear; even I will carry, and will deliver you.

Isaiah 46:4 (KJV)

These are some of the promises of the Scriptures. But the Bible is literally full of them, promise after promise after promise. Generations have proven them true, and so can you. God's promises are treasures waiting to be discovered.

7

Pooh Sticks

You were running well. Who hindered you from obeying the truth?

Galatians 5:7 (ESV)

A drawing of Winnie the Pooh as he played pooh sticks with Piglet and Christopher Robin was sold by auction house Sotheby's for more than £300,000. The illustration by E. H. Shepard, first published in 1928 and one of the most famous images of Pooh, had been in a private collection for more than forty years.

Pooh sticks was invented by English author A. A. Milne who wrote the Winnie the Pooh stories. The sport first came to prominence when it was described in the author's book *The House at Pooh Corner*. In the traditional version of pooh sticks, the participants must drop a stick simultaneously on the upstream side of a bridge and run to the other side. The winner is the player whose stick first appears on the other side of the bridge. Alternatively, players may decide upon a starting point on a river and a finish line farther downstream. The winner is the player whose stick first passes the finishing point. It is generally agreed that the stick must be made of organic materials, preferably willow, and it must be dropped, not thrown, into the water to avoid disqualification.

Here's how it all began. One day, when Pooh bear was just walking along the bridge with a fir cone in his paw, in his own world, not looking where he was going (probably thinking about honey), he tripped over something. This made the fir-cone jerk out of his paw into the river.

"Bother," said Pooh, as it floated slowly under the bridge. So Pooh went to get another fir cone, but then thought that he would just look at the river instead, because it was a peaceful sort of day. So, he lay down and looked at it and suddenly, there was his fir-cone slipping away too. "That's funny," said Pooh. "I dropped it on the other side, and it came out on this side! I wonder if it would do it again?" And he went back for some more fir-cones. It did. It kept on doing it. Then he dropped two in at once, and leant over the bridge to see which of them would come out first; and one of them did; but as they were both the same size, he didn't know if it was the one which he wanted to win or the other one.

> *And that was the beginning of the game called Pooh sticks, which Pooh invented, and which he and his friends used to play on the edge of the Forest. But they played with sticks instead of fir-cones, because they were easier to mark.*[39]

I played it with my friends as a child and was told that it's all about learning to win and lose gracefully. Really? We were so competitive – we streamlined our branches, checked for the fastest flowing side void of algae and argued over whose stick was the winning one and whose got stuck behind the stone. We all wanted to win the race. The Bible tells us:

> *...let us also lay aside every weight, and sin which clings so closely, and let us run with endurance the race that is set before us, looking to Jesus...*
>
> *Hebrews 12:1-2 (ESV)*

We need to streamline our lives. Just like in the game pooh sticks, our stick may flow well until obstructed. The Greek word for "hindered" in today's verse literally means 'to elbow someone out of the race or impede one's course'. What or who is hindering us from running our race or impeding our course? Streamline, get in the flow and run in such a way that you may win.[40]

---

[39] A.A. Milne; *Winnie the Pooh* (1926)
[40] See 1 Corinthians 9:24

8

Paper Town

Don't copy the behaviour and customs of this world, but let God transform you into a new person by changing the way you think. Then you will learn to know God's will for you, which is good and pleasing and perfect.

Romans 12:2 (NLT)

What is a paper town? That was the question I tried to resolve as I tuned in to the radio yesterday amid a discussion about paper towns. I had never heard of the term before and I was curious. Apparently, a paper town is a fake town created by cartographers to protect the copyright of their map. Mapmakers put fake streets, fake towns and fake bridges in their maps, so if they see those same fake places appearing on someone else's map, they immediately know that they've been robbed. The paper towns and trap streets help mapmakers prove that copyright infringement has occurred. It's an age-old practice to keep copycats at bay.

Our verse today tells us not to copy the behaviour and customs of this world. That's not our purpose. Instead of blending into our copycat culture and becoming carbon copies of one another, we are meant to be unique. That begins with the realisation of David who wrote:

...I am fearfully and wonderfully made.

Psalm 139:14 (KJV)

God carefully mixed the DNA recipe that created you. David praised God for this incredible personal attention to detail in designing each of us:

Thank you for making me so wonderfully complex! Your workmanship is marvellous.

Psalm 139:14 (NLT)

In a world of roughly seven billion people you have a unique calling on your life and unique gifting to make that calling possible. You are essentially one of a kind. God has created each of us differently right down to our fingertips. No one else has been given exactly the same makeup as God has given you. I admire the title of a book by John Mason which states, "You were born an original. Don't die a copy."

The Bible tells us:

> *God has given each of us the ability to do certain things well.*
>
> *Romans 12:6 (TLB)*

Furthermore, it instructs us:

> *…whatever you do, do it all for the glory of God.*
>
> *1 Corinthians 10:31 (NIV)*

In other words, each one of us has the ability to do certain things well and we should use the unique abilities God has given us for His glory. What are some of the unique traits you possess – skills, strengths, passions? Take an inventory and consider your list with fresh eyes today. How could these traits be used to connect others to God and intentionally glorify Him?

9

Zip Your Lip

Set a guard over my mouth, LORD;
  keep watch over the door of my lips.

Psalm 141:3 (NIV)

Who remembers the loveable characters Zippy, Bungle and George? They appeared in a show called Rainbow. Bungle (my favourite) was a bulky brown teddy bear who griped about the other members. George was a massive pink hippopotamus, known for his shyness. Zippy was a rather loud character, always wanting to be the centre of attention, and had a zip for his mouth. Whenever he 'mouthed off', the other puppets zipped his mouth shut.

Zippy came to mind as I pondered today's verse. David did not want anything harmful to leave his mouth. Proverbs 10:19 offers some similar advice:

Too much talk leads to sin.
  Be sensible and keep your mouth shut.

Proverbs 10:19 (NLT)

Instead of speaking rashly, unadvisedly, improperly, we should keep our mouths shut. We all know that it is not good to gossip, gripe, deceive, slander, criticise etc. But how about the following admission: "I am an interrupter. I am a finisher-of-sentences. I am a talk-over-another-person kind of person. I am a how-can-I-turn-this-conversation-back-to-me participant. I am what some call a 'conversational narcissist'." The truth is, we all have problems with what we say and how we say it. How we need the advice, "Be sensible and keep your mouth shut."

I was once given the following challenge. If you were given £10 for every kind and edifying word you've spoken, but penalised £10 for every unkind, hurtful word you've uttered, and then bought a house with the balance, what kind of home would you now have or would you be homeless? Our prayer must be that of the Psalmist: "Set a guard over my mouth, Lord; keep watch over the door of my lips."

10

Refined and Defined

And not only this, but we also exult in our tribulations, knowing that tribulation brings about perseverance; and perseverance, proven character; and proven character, hope; and hope does not disappoint, because the love of God has been poured out within our hearts through the Holy Spirit who was given to us.

Romans 5:3-5 (NASB)

We use the word 'character' in many ways. In my neck of the woods we would say, "He's a bit of a character," meaning that he has a style of his own and captures your attention in either a negative or positive way. Watching the programme *Escape to the Country*, I hear the house-hunters asking for a period property "with character". In theatrical terms we have different characters in a play, for example, Ebenezer Scrooge is a character in *A Christmas Carol* by Charles Dickens. We watch cartoon characters with our children. We sometimes say, "He's got lots of character," or, "It was totally out of character for him." Tweets on the social media outlet *Twitter* will now allow 280 characters to be typed. The word 'character' is used in so many ways. The origin of the word 'character' is from the Greek word *kharakter* referring to 'a defining quality, a distinguishing quality'.

Our verses today speak of proven character.

Tribulation → Perseverance → Character → Hope.

Perseverance produces proven character. This is a single word in the Greek *(dokime)* which refers to something which has passed the test. It comes out approved. It is the quality of being tried and approved. *Dokime* in secular Greek was used to describe metals that had been tested and were determined to be pure. The idea of *dokime* is that when you put the metal through a fiery test and everything base has been purged out of it, you call the metal 'proven', 'authentic' or 'genuine'. When you go through a trial trusting in God, your faith becomes proven. You've been through the test and passed. You know by experience that you can lean on His faithfulness. It is through the storms of life that our character is refined, shaped and moulded. Our refining moments can indeed become our defining moments. Trials are part and parcel of living in this fallen world. Paul, who weathered many trials, says that he exults in his tribulations.[41] Why? He knows that his character is being honed and proven. James says the same thing:

> *Consider it all joy, my brethren, when you encounter various trials, knowing that the testing of your faith produces endurance. And let endurance have its perfect result, so that you may be perfect and complete, lacking in nothing.*
>
> *James 1:2-4 (NASB)*

Again, he says:

> *Blessed is a man who perseveres under trial; for once he has been approved [dokimos], he will receive the crown of life which the Lord has promised to those who love Him.*
>
> *James 1:12 (NASB)*

The bottom line is that trials reveal who you really are – and, more importantly, where your allegiance lies. Both Paul and James knew that a by-product of suffering was character development. Paul said:

> *Knowing that suffering produces...*
>
> *Romans 5:3 (ESV)*

Suffering does something, accomplishes something. It is productive. It refined and defines us. Now that we know the process, let's remain steadfast and see the distinguishing quality of God's work in us.

---

[41] See Romans 5:3

11

The Beauty of Brokenness

The sacrifices of God are a broken spirit;
A broken and a contrite heart, O God, You will not despise.

Psalm 51:17 (NASB)

When I hear the word "broken", Royal Doulton horses come to mind. On our mantlepiece at home my Mum's Royal Doulton horses had pride of place. They survived my childhood years but shortly into adolescence I clumsily swiped one with my sleeve and it landed on the hearth in smithereens. My image of the word "broken" therefore had negative connotations. Add to that a broken arm (from riding a horse) and 'being broke' as a student and you can see how this wasn't my favourite word.

However, I learned that there are other more positive ways to apply the word. It is only when a horse is broken that it becomes useful to its owner. It is only when a shell is broken that the chick can emerge and experience life at large. In the Bible it was only when the pitchers were broken and the light shone out that Israel experienced victory.[42] It was only when the alabaster box was broken that the ointment poured out on Jesus.[43] It was only as the bread was broken that Jesus fed the huge crowd.[44] There are some things in our lives that need to be broken: pride, self-will, stubbornness, sin. God must break us of our self-dependence, self-confidence and self-sufficiency so that we realise we can fully depend on Him. That part which wants its own way, seeks its own glory and stands up for its own rights at last bows its head to God's will in brokenness. It is the shattering of self-will, the stripping of self-reliance and independence from God, the softening of the soil of the heart.

On the night before He died, Jesus broke the bread and said:

---

[42] See Judges 7:18-19
[43] See Mark 14:3
[44] See Matthew 14:10

And he took bread, and when he had given thanks, he broke it and gave it to them, saying, "This is my body, which is given for you. Do this in remembrance of me."

Luke 22:19 (ESV)

He went all the way to Calvary to die so that we can live. His death has made it possible for broken, sinful humanity to be reconciled to God and be healed. Brokenness brings us closer to God.

The Lord is nigh unto them that are of a broken heart.

Psalm 34:18 (KJV)

He is repulsed by pride but attracted to brokenness. In brokenness we get a new perspective of His mercy and provision, a more complete comprehension of His unconditional love, an overwhelming need of a Saviour, godly sorrow and repentance. Brokenness removes the focus from the clay jar.

...we have this treasure in jars of clay to show that this all-surpassing power is from God and not from us.

2 Corinthians 4:7 (NIV)

Many are humbled, but not humble. Many are low, but not lowly. Many are heartbroken, but not broken. May we have "a broken spirit; a broken and a contrite heart."

12

The Story of the Sandwich

Praise the LORD.
Praise God in His sanctuary;
 praise Him in his mighty heavens.
Praise Him for His acts of power;
 praise Him for His surpassing greatness.
Praise Him with the sounding of the trumpet,
 praise Him with the harp and lyre,
praise Him with timbrel and dancing,
 praise Him with the strings and pipe,
praise Him with the clash of cymbals,
 praise Him with resounding cymbals.
Let everything that has breath praise the LORD.
Praise the LORD.

Psalm 150:1-6 (NIV)

What we now widely recognise as a sandwich is thought to have originated in England during the 18th century. It was named after John Montagu, 4th Earl of Sandwich, an eighteenth-century English aristocrat. It is said that in approximately 1762, he asked for meat to be served between slices of bread, and others began to order "the same as Sandwich".

What's your favourite kind of sandwich? What is your ideal filling between two slices of bread? What is your favourite lunchtime staple? A sandwich is portable, open to any interpretation and as simple or as elaborate as the mood permits. Peanut butter, egg and onion, cheese and cherry tomato, tuna and mayo, BLT, jam, crisps, deli meat and salad leaves, chicken and cucumber – the choice is yours.

The last Psalm, number 150, is like a sandwich. Sandwiched between the words "Praise the LORD!" David wraps up the book with a glorious psalm of praise, an eloquent, passionate plea to give God the praise due to Him. The Psalm begins and ends with the Hebrew word *hallelujah,* meaning, 'Praise the LORD!' Thirteen times this Hebrew word is mentioned in Psalm 150. Thirteen times in six short verses the psalmist calls us to "praise the LORD".

The sandwich filling of Psalm 150 is a synopsis of praise.

Where is the Lord to be praised? Everywhere! No limits. In His sanctuary. In His mighty heavens. We can and should praise God wherever we are.

Why should we praise the Lord? Praise Him for His acts of power; praise Him for His surpassing greatness. We praise for what He does and Who He is. Breathe in His grace; breathe out His praise.

How should we praise the Lord? With everything we have!

Who is to praise the Lord? Everyone! Anyone who has breath!

You take approximately 23,000 breaths every day, but when was the last time you thanked God for one of them? I wonder how many of us can honestly say, "Praising God characterises my daily life." I challenge you to lift up your voice and declare God's excellencies today. Where? Anywhere and everywhere. Why? Because of his power and greatness. How? In any and every possible way. Who? Everyone who has breath.

Everywhere. For everything. With everything. Everyone. Begin and end your day praising the Lord. Let your life be filled with praise.

13

Gone Phishing

...we are not ignorant of his schemes.

2 Corinthians 2:11 (NASB)

The history of the term 'phishing' is not entirely clear. One common explanation for the term is that 'phishing' is a homophone of 'fishing', and is so named because phishing scams use lures to catch unsuspecting victims. Phishing is a form of fraud in which an attacker masquerades as a reputable entity or established enterprise in email or other communication channels. The purpose is to obtain sensitive information such as usernames, passwords, credit card details and bank account numbers for malicious reasons.

While some phishing emails are poorly written and clearly fake, others are difficult to distinguish from authentic messages; a phishing email can include corporate logos and other identifying graphics and data For most phishing attacks, whether carried out by email or some other medium, the objective is to get the victim to follow a link that appears to go to a legitimate web resource, but that actually takes the victim to a malicious web resource.

Phishing emails are blindly sent to thousands, if not millions, of recipients. By spamming large groups of people, the 'phisher' counts on the email being read by a percentage of people who actually have an account with the legitimate company being spoofed in the email and corresponding webpage. You have probably received emails claiming to be from your bank asking you to "verify" your credit card. They're from fraudsters phishing for your information. These scams succeed because they look like the real thing and catch you off guard when you're not expecting it.

The enemy, the devil, is a scammer and a schemer according to the Bible. Jesus said:

"Satan desired to have you, that he may sift you like wheat."

Luke 22:31 (KJV)

He is referred to as a liar and the father of lies. He has blinded the minds of the unbelievers, to keep them from seeing the light of the gospel of the glory of Christ. He disguises himself as an angel of light.

In Ephesians 6:11 we are told to put on the whole armour of God that we might be able "to stand against the wiles of the devil"[45].

The word "wiles" is sometimes translated "tactics"[46] or "schemes"[47] or "strategies"[48]. 'Strategy' is the carefully arranged plan to deceive and outwit others. The devil's primary work is deception, and thus the words "wiles", "tactics", "schemes" and "strategies" are all appropriate.

It is time to grow in wisdom, apply God's truth, test the spirits, discern all things and stand firm in faith.

> *Your enemy the devil prowls around like a roaring lion looking for someone to devour. Resist him, standing firm in the faith.*
>
> *1 Peter 5:8 (NIV)*

We must follow Paul's example and not be ignorant of Satan's devices. Let's not be outwitted or phished by the enemy of our souls by compromising our identity in Christ. Avoid links or attachments which would lead you astray. Don't download harmful software that would corrupt your system. Stay vigilant.

---

[45] NKJV
[46] e.g. HCSB
[47] e.g. NIV
[48] e.g. NLT

14

Are You a Good Listener?

My dear brothers and sisters, take note of this: Everyone should be quick to listen, slow to speak and slow to become angry.

James 1:19 (NIV)

I have been reflecting lately on how important – and how difficult – it is to listen. Research shows that the average person listens with only twenty-five percent efficiency, meaning there's a lot we're letting go in one ear and out the other. I remember being told that God gave us two ears and one mouth so we should do twice as much listening as speaking. I know that sometimes we get this verse reversed and are quick to speak but slow to listen.

To be a good listener we need to be:

Attentive. A good listener is attentive, making good eye contact and listening not only to the words but also to the feeling of what is being conveyed. Watch for non-verbal communication and tone of voice. Learn the art of reading what people are really saying beyond their words. This can help you be more compassionate and understanding of people.

Do not interrupt. Allow the people you are communicating with to share their feelings and thoughts uninterrupted. Don't hijack the conversation. A good listener is not waiting for their chance to get a word in, treating the 'period of listening' as a pause in their 'monologue'. You've probably encountered people who frequently interrupt, take over the conversation and use the audience as a platform for talking about themselves or sharing their knowledge or expertise. Poor listening diminishes the other person, while good listening values the individual.

Be patient and don't presume. Bonhoeffer[49] gives us something to avoid: "a kind of listening with half an ear that presumes already to know

---

[49] Dietrich Bonhoeffer; *Life Together: The Classic Exploration of Christian Community*

what the other person has to say." This, he says, "is an impatient, inattentive listening, that ... is only waiting for a chance to speak." Perhaps we're half-eared in our listening because our attention is divided by our external surroundings or our internal spotlight on self. The Bible tells that genuine love looks not only to its own interests, but also the interests of others.[50] It is patient and kind.[51] It also states that it is the fool who "takes no pleasure in understanding, but only in expressing his opinion"[52], and thus "gives an answer before he hears"[53].

Let's "be quick to listen" today.

---

[50] See Philippians 2:4
[51] See 1 Corinthians 13:4
[52] Proverbs 18:2 (ESV)
[53] Proverbs 18:13 (ESV)

15

Our Train of Thought

We demolish arguments and every pretension that sets itself up against the knowledge of God, and we take captive every thought to make it obedient to Christ.

2 Corinthians 10:5 (NIV)

[Jesus] knew what they were thinking.

Luke 6:8 (NASB)

Spam. As a term for junk email, 'spam' entered the Oxford English Dictionary in 1998. But why are unsolicited irrelevant email messages called spam? Skip down to the second meaning in the dictionary and we get a clue: "A tinned meat product made mainly from ham." Hormel Foods introduced Spam luncheon meat in 1937. It's a simple shortening of 'spiced ham' or 'shoulders of pork and ham'. Much to the chagrin of Hormel Foods, the term spam has today come to mean junk e-mail. How did the term get this meaning? I went on a mission of etymological research. Apparently, it came from a skit by *Monty Python's Flying Circus.* In the sketch, a restaurant serves all its food with lots of spam, and the waitress repeats the word several times in describing how much spam is in the items. When she does this, a group of Vikings (don't ask) in the corner start a song, "Spam, spam, spam, spam, spam, spam, spam, spam, lovely spam! Wonderful spam!" They continue until told to shut up. Thus the meaning of the term: something that keeps repeating and repeating to great annoyance.

No-one likes unnecessary junk in their mailbox. But what about the unnecessary junk in the inbox of our minds? Our verse today talks of how we need to "take captive every thought to make it obedient to Christ". The Greek word for "take captive" means 'to control, to conquer, to bring into submission'. Take captive every thought. Through media outlets we are daily bombarded with thoughts of materialism, hedonism, atheism, secularism and many other 'isms' which we need to block. Thoughts stream into our minds through the social media websites we browse, the reality shows we watch and the gossip we hear. Paul says that we must "demolish arguments and every pretension that sets itself up against the knowledge of God". Trash them. Unsubscribe to thoughts of worry and negativity. Use the Word of God as a filter to stop contrary information from getting into your heart.

We have to be careful what we let in and what we allow to influence us. Paul advised:

> *Finally, brethren, whatever is true, whatever is honorable, whatever is right, whatever is pure, whatever is lovely, whatever is of good repute, if there is any excellence and if anything worthy of praise, dwell on these things.*
>
> *Philippians 4:8 (NASB)*

Paul tells us:

> *...do not be conformed to this world, but be transformed by the renewing of your mind...*
>
> *Romans 12:2 (NASB)*

We are to renew our minds with God's truths, and not continue to think the way the world thinks or the way the devil wants us to think. Make a commitment to monitor your thinking patterns and stop the spam.

16

Not Everything is Beneficial

"Everything is permissible for me" – but not everything is beneficial. "Everything is permissible for me" – but I will not be mastered by anything.

1 Corinthians 6:12 (NIV)

*I*n Chapter 6 of 1 Corinthians, Paul is dealing with a church where some very poor choices are being made. There are people in the church that are living in a worldly way and he wants them to learn how to function within the framework of liberty. In verse 12, "Everything is permissible for me" is in quotation marks because this is what the people were saying. This was a slogan the Corinthians were using. Paul had to instruct them that not everything is beneficial. Or as the KJV translation says, "...all things are not expedient." The Greek word for "expedient" means 'profitable', 'for your good'.

Paul is correcting the Corinthians' misconception of our liberty as believers under the New Covenant. Yes, we have freedom, but we must measure our choices by their spiritual benefit.

Later in 1 Corinthians 10:23 Paul writes:

"All things are lawful," but not all things are helpful. "All things are lawful," but not all things build up.

1 Corinthians 10:23 (ESV)

In the Greek, the first part of this verse is identical to the first part of 1 Corinthians 6:12. At the end of 10:23, "build up" comes from the Greek word *oikodomeo*, which literally means 'to build a house'. So, all things are lawful but not all things build up the house.

Not everything is beneficial. As I need to eat gluten-free food, all food is permissible for me but it's evident that all food is not beneficial for me. It might not be food that is an issue with you; it could be another area of life where you struggle with things not helpful to you. Buying things is permissible... but when you are neck-deep in bills, is that beneficial?

Golf, biking, hiking, social networking, watching television, fishing etc... all are permissible and morally neutral activities, but if we do them to the neglect of our families and spiritual life, they are not beneficial.

Let's check our choices. Are they beneficial? Are they expedient? Are they constructive and edifying? All things are permissible, but not all things are beneficial.

17

North, East, South, West

For as high as the heavens are above the earth,
  so great is his steadfast love toward those who fear him;
as far as the east is from the west,
  so far does he remove our transgressions from us.

Psalm 103:11-12 (ESV)

was perusing the chapter titles in a book of perplexing questions. For example:

- Why are there no 'B' batteries in the shops?
- At a movie theatre which armrest is yours?
- Why are the numbers on a calculator and a phone reversed?

The one which caught my eye asked, "How far east can you go before you're heading west?" The reason it got my attention was because it reminded me of today's reading. God says that He has separated my sins from me as far as the east is from the west. Rather than treating us as our sins deserve, God removes our sins from us.

The reality is that there is no place at which east meets west. Suddenly, that verse takes on a whole new meaning. If God had chosen the words "north from south" that would mean that there would be some eventual point at which we would meet up with our sins again. But by carefully choosing the words "east ... from ... west", God was showing us that there will never be a point in the future where we will meet our sins again. The distance from north to south is measurable. In every sphere there are north and south poles – both fixed points; and on the earth the distance between them is roughly twelve thousand miles. Had the psalmist said, "As far as the north is from the south," our conceptions would have been thus limited. It is otherwise with the east and the west. There are no eastern and western poles. From every point alike in the circuit of the world, the east extends in one direction, the west in the other.

If you travel far enough north, you will eventually end up going south when you make the turn at the north pole and start heading back down the other side of the globe. On the other hand, if you travel west then you just keep going to the west and you'll never start travelling east. Eastward travel and westward travel continue without end. Thus, there is an infinite distance between east and west.

God says:

> *"I, even I, am He who blots out your transgressions, for my own sake, and remembers your sins no more."*
>
> *Isaiah 43:25 (NIV)*

Hebrews 10 explains how Jesus' sacrifice on the cross for sin was a once-and-for-all sacrifice. Unlike the sacrificial system of the Old Testament, in which sacrifices were continually made for sin, Jesus paid for sin once. His payment was complete.

> *Every priest stands daily ministering and offering time after time the same sacrifices, which can never take away sins; but He, having offered one sacrifice for sins for all time, sat down at the right hand of God.*
>
> *Hebrews 10:11-12 (NASB)*

In verse 17 God says:

> *AND THEIR SINS AND THEIR LAWLESS DEEDS I WILL REMEMBER NO MORE.*
>
> *Hebrews 10:17 (NASB)*

Refuse to live in condemnation and begin to walk in the newness of Christ with freedom in knowing that through the cross, believers under the new covenant receive God's total forgiveness!

18

Reflecting God's Radiance

Those who look to him are radiant...

Psalm 34:5 (NIV)

When someone wants to take your photograph and you face the camera, how do you respond? Do you smile? Pose? Blink unintentionally? Make a funny face? Pout? Across Europe, the most common expression heard when someone is taking a snap is, "Say, 'Cheese!'" to which the perfect response is a wide, toothy grin as the subject replies, "Cheese!"

But does "Cheese!" really produce the radiant smile? Not everyone says, "Cheese!" In France some say, "Oustiti" ('little monkey'). In Italy you may be asked to say, "Famiglia" ('family'). In Spain, "Patatas" ('potatoes'); in Poland, "Marmolada" ('marmalade') and in Holland, "Zeg Eens Kaas" ('say cheese'). All are attempts by photographers to produce a radiant smile in their subject.

The Bible tells us, "Those who look to Him are radiant." The Hebrew word translated for us as "radiant" means 'to shine, beam, emit rays of light, glow'. If you Google "How to be radiant?" the answers will include:

- make sure that you have at least five portions of fruit and vegetables every day;
- drink lots of water as it moisturises your skin;
- get seven hours of sleep;
- eat walnuts like almonds;
- whiten your teeth.

But what does the Bible say? It says those who "look to *him*" are radiant. We understand the pronoun "him" as referring to the word "LORD" in the preceding verse. That's the secret of true radiance.

In Exodus 34:29 we are told:

When Moses came down from Mount Sinai with the two tablets of the covenant law in his hands, he was not aware that his face was radiant because he had spoken with the LORD.

Exodus 34:29 (NIV)

He had been with the Lord. God's glory was shining from Moses' face. Moses was so relationally close to God that his face reflected God's radiance.

The Bible says that Jesus is coming back for "a radiant church, without stain or wrinkle or any other blemish, but holy and blameless"[54]. Are we reflecting God's radiance?

In the Aaronic blessing in Numbers 6:24-26 it states:

"The LORD bless you and keep you;
The LORD make his face shine upon you
And be gracious to you;
The LORD turn his face toward you
And give you peace."

Numbers 6:24-26 (NKJV)

"The LORD make his face shine upon you." Radiance is the outward evidence of an inward reality. You and I are a reflection of where we spend our time and with whom we spend our time. So, when we spend time in the presence of the Lord in worship, when we look into His Word, then the light of His presence and Word shine upon us and through us. Look intently into His Word and "gaze upon the beauty of the Lord"[55]. Then shine! Isaiah 60:1 in the Amplified Bible tells us:

Arise [from the depression and prostration in which circumstances have kept you – rise to a new life]! Shine (be radiant with the glory of the Lord), for your light has come, and the glory of the Lord has risen upon you!

Isaiah 60:1 (AMPC)

---

[54] Ephesians 5:27 (NIV)
[55] Psalm 27:4 (ESV)

19

Gospel in a Nutshell

For God so loved the world that He gave His only begotten Son, that whoever believes in Him should not perish but have everlasting life.

John 3:16 (NKJV)

*H*ave you ever heard of Achoo Syndrome? Have you ever looked at a bright light/sun and had a sneezing fit? Sneezing when you look at a bright light is caused by a genetic reflex called Autosomal Compelling Helio-Ophthalmic Outburst syndrome – which is also known by its cool acronym ACHOO, fittingly the word to represent the sound of a sneeze.

I love stumbling upon helpful ways of remembering things. Let me share one of my favourites from the Bible. We often see signs and banners at sporting events that say "John 3:16". The Gospel of John, chapter 3, verse 16, is one of the all-time beloved and well-known verses in the entire Bible.

It tells us of the love God has for us and the extent of that love – so great that He sacrificed His only Son on our behalf. It teaches us that anyone who believes in Jesus Christ, God's Son, will "not perish but have everlasting life". The Protestant reformer Martin Luther called it "the gospel in miniature". Biblical Commentator William Barclay wrote that it is "the very essence of the Gospel". John 3:16 explains the entire Bible. The verse condenses all of God's plan from the beginning of time and throughout Scripture into this tiny 'nutshell' of a verse. It is the gospel message in simplest form. In fact, look carefully and you will spot the very word 'GOSPEL' hidden in the verse.

GOSPEL: God so loved the world that He gave His Only begotten Son, that whoever believes in Him should not Perish but have Everlasting Life.

The word 'gospel' means 'good news'. In the Greek New Testament, "gospel" is the translation of the Greek noun *euangelion* ('good news') and the verb *euangelizo* meaning 'to bring or announce good news'. It is the good news, the greatest news this world has ever heard and needs to hear. "[John 3:16] is a twenty-six word parade of hope: beginning with God, ending with Life, and urging us to do the same," wrote Max Lucado.

Another helpful outline to help us remember it is:

For God (the greatest Giver)
so loved (the greatest motive)
the world (the greatest need)
that He gave (the greatest act)
His only begotten Son (the greatest gift)
that whosoever (the greatest invitation)
believeth (the greatest decision)
in Him (the greatest Person)
believeth in Him (the greatest opportunity)
should not perish (the greatest deliverance)
but (the greatest difference)
have (the greatest certainty)
everlasting life (the greatest possession).

John 3:16 – the gospel in a nutshell. So let us go into all the world, and preach the GOSPEL to every creature.[56]

---

[56] See Mark 16:15

20

There for You

Fear not, for I am with you;
Be not dismayed, for I am your God.
I will strengthen you,
Yes, I will help you.
I will uphold you with my righteous right hand.

Isaiah 41:10

Today as I drove out of town I got caught in some traffic congestion as a large SPAR lorry attempted to reverse into an extremely tight entrance. As I sat back and watched the driver skilfully manoeuvre his vehicle, my attention was riveted on the side of the lorry which bore the SPAR slogan, "There for you." The website tells you:

> *SPAR has always been there for you. Packed with all the essentials for everyday living, we're your friendly neighbourhood store – convenient, close and always open when you need us.*

Operating here for over fifty years, SPAR is one of the country's largest convenience retail groups. The name was originally DE SPAR, an acronym of the Dutch phrase, 'Door Eendrachtig Samenwerken Profiteren Allen Regelmatig.' It translates as, 'We all benefit from joint cooperation.' The acronym was chosen in order to resonate with the verb 'spar' or 'spaar' which means 'save [money]' in Dutch. To symbolise the strength of this organisation, Adriaan van Well used the fir tree as part of the 'DE SPAR' logo. In Dutch, 'de spar' means a fir tree.

What a message! There for you... We all benefit from joint cooperation... Save...

Sometimes we feel alone when we experience trials and difficulties in life. At these times it is necessary to remember Who is always there for us. You can rest in the fact that "God is with you wherever you go."[57] That should strengthen your resolve and calm your fears. In similar words to the Psalmist we can say:

I will fear no evil,
For You are with me.

Psalm 23:4 (NKJV)

The One who saves us, Jesus Christ, has said:

"And behold, I am with you always, to the end of the age."

Matthew 28:20 (ESV)

He is there for us today, tomorrow and forever. In every season of life He is there for you. In every valley He is your very present help. In the fiery furnace you'll find Him. See the slogan "there for you" everywhere you go and be reassured that He is all you need.

---

[57] Joshua 1:9 (NKJV)

21

Are You Resting on Your Laurels?

What is more, I consider everything a loss because of the surpassing worth of knowing Christ Jesus my Lord...

Philippians 3:8 (NIV)

The idea of resting on your laurels dates back to athletes of ancient Greece. Victorious athletes at the Ancient Greek Pythian Games were given wreaths made of the aromatic laurel leaves as a symbol of their triumph, and the Romans later adopted the practice and presented wreaths to military commanders who won important battles. Venerable Greeks and Romans, or 'laureates', were thus able to 'rest on their laurels' by basking in the glory of past achievements. The negative connotation, and the saying, only came about after the decline of the Ancient Greek and Roman empires. Since the 1800s it has been used for those who are overly satisfied with past triumphs.

Paul says:

> *If anyone else has reason to be confident in the flesh, I have more: circumcised on the eighth day, a member of the people of Israel, of the tribe of Benjamin, a Hebrew born of Hebrews; as to the law, a Pharisee; as to zeal, a persecutor of the church; as to righteousness under the law, blameless.*
>
> *Philippians 3:4-6 (NRSV)*

Paul had an illustrious past. He had impeccable credentials. He was a model Pharisee. He was a religious connoisseur. If anyone could have rested on his spiritual laurels it was the apostle Paul. In the past, Paul had been proud of those credentials and accomplishments. But now, because of Christ, his perspective had changed entirely.

Paul is speaking in Philippians 3 of the life-changing experience he had when he encountered the risen Christ on the road to Damascus and became a follower of Christ. He writes:

But whatever things were gain to me, those things I have counted as loss for the sake of Christ.

Philippians 3:7 (NASB)

Using the language of the accounting ledger, Paul says that what he previously regarded as gains he came to regard as losses because of his newfound relationship with Christ. He puts it emphatically:

More than that, I count all things to be loss in view of the surpassing value of knowing Christ Jesus my Lord.

Philippians 3:8 (NASB)

In Paul's life, what he thought were assets were really liabilities! He says, "I regard them as rubbish."[58] The term Paul wrote is derived from the Greek *skubalon*, used only here in the entire New Testament. The word refers to excrement. In short, Paul is describing his great and noteworthy human achievements using the worst word picture he could share with his audience. All that mattered to Paul was Christ; everything else was not merely less valuable – it was utter garbage. His advice to us: shred your religious résumé. What do you boast in? Where does your confidence lie? Our 'good works' apart from Christ are putrid in God's nostrils. They cannot earn salvation or even maintain salvation. Do an accounting of your life and figure out what matters – and what doesn't. To Paul, nothing else mattered in comparison to Christ. Don't rest on your laurels – rest in the Lord.

---

[58] Philippians 3:8 (NRSV)

22

Practise Playing Second Fiddle

Love from the center of who you are; don't fake it. Run for dear life from evil; hold on for dear life to good. Be good friends who love deeply; practice playing second fiddle.

Romans 12:10 (MSG)

I'm quite surprised at how many idioms involve the word 'fiddle'. As a verb, 'to fiddle' means not only 'to play the violin', but also 'to fidget with your hands in a nervous or restless way'. Colloquially, and often followed by the preposition 'around', to fiddle means 'to squander time'. It can also be an act of defrauding meaning 'to cheat or falsify'. 'To be fit as a fiddle' means to be in extremely good health. 'A face as long as a fiddle' is a dismal face. 'Hang up your fiddle' means to retire from business or give up an undertaking. 'There's many a good tune played on an old fiddle' means that someone's abilities do not depend on their age. 'Fiddle while Rome burns' means to take little or no productive action during a crisis.

How about the phrase 'playing second fiddle'? Unsurprisingly, the expression is generally held to have its origins in the world of music. In early orchestras the most prominent and high-profile member of the orchestra was the musician who played the lead or first violin. Naturally, there would also be other violinists in the string section of the orchestra, but these would not be as important or honoured as the lead violinist. These other violinists became known as 'second fiddles' and the expression has now become firmly established in the language.

Leonard Bernstein, the celebrated orchestra conductor, was asked, "What is the hardest instrument to play?" He replied without hesitation, "Second fiddle. I can always get plenty of first violinists, but to find one who plays second violin with as much enthusiasm or second French horn or second flute, now that's a problem. And yet if no one plays second, we have no harmony." I suspect God finds that to be true in His kingdom as well. God's church only functions properly if people work in the background or behind the scenes playing second fiddle without recognition.

In Romans 12:10 Paul instructed us to practise playing second fiddle. To practise something is to work at it frequently in an effort to excel in it. In his commentary, Charles Spurgeon wrote that this kind of love is "putting another before yourself, aspiring after the second place, rather than the first". John the Baptist knew what this was like. He had a large following. Then came Jesus. I wonder how John felt about stepping aside and pointing his disciples to Jesus? He said of Jesus:

"He must increase and I must decrease."

John 3:30 (CEB)

John understood that he was to "prepare the way"[59] and he was willing to lose himself in the task of doing that and pointing his disciples to Jesus, the Lamb of God.

How good are you at playing second fiddle?

---

[59] Matthew 3:3 (NKJV)

23

A Carrot, Egg or Coffee Bean?

Why am I so depressed?
Why this turmoil within me?
Put your hope in God, for I will still praise Him,
my Savior and my God.

Psalm 42:11 (HCSB)

For many people, heating water over the stove is an important part of their tea-making ritual. I must admit that while I mostly use my electric kettle, I occasionally put my cast iron kettle on the stove and listen for that lovely whistling noise which tells me that my water is ready to use for the perfect cup of tea or coffee. The hotter the water gets, the louder it whistles!

We believers should be like those old whistling kettles, still singing when we are up to our necks in hot water! Incarcerated in a Philippian dungeon, their hands and feet locked in stocks, their backs flogged, we read of the response of Paul and Silas:

At midnight Paul and Silas were ... singing hymns to God ...
Suddenly there was a great earthquake ... the foundations of
the prison were shaken; and immediately all the doors were
opened and everyone's chains were loosed.

Acts 16:25-26 (NKJV)

Up to their necks in hot water, they chose to sing.

I remember reading about the different types of cedar trees and one was called the 'humming' cedar. When the winds would blow, especially on a cold winter night, the humming cedar with its bell-shaped leaves would give off a melodious humming sound. This cedar loves the wind. The stronger the wind blows, the more the humming cedar hums. Interestingly, the Psalmist said that the righteous man shall "grow like a cedar of Lebanon"[60]. When we find ourselves in hot water and when the winds whip up a storm in our lives, how do we respond?

I was once asked, "Are you a carrot, an egg or a coffee bean?" I was given an illustration of what happens when each of these objects face the same adversity: a pot of hot water. The carrot became limp and lost its strength. The egg became hardened. The coffee beans were unique, however. After they were in the boiling water, they changed the water and spread a delicious aroma.

How do you handle adversity? Keep on praising, keep on hoping. The psalmist in Psalm 42 shared his despair:

> *Why, my soul, are you downcast?*
> *Why so disturbed within me?*
>
> *Psalm 42:11a (NIV)*

Then he instructed himself to hope in God.

> *Put your hope in God,*
> *for I will yet praise Him,*
> *my Savior and my God.*
>
> *Psalm 42:11b (NIV)*

The expression "I will yet praise Him" signifies an inner determination and a forward-facing outlook. He persistently, continually and repeatedly praises the Lord.

When Israel was outnumbered by the enemy, God told them to put a choir in front of the army and march into battle. And it worked!

> *When they began ... to praise, the LORD set ambushes against the [enemy].*
>
> *2 Chronicles 20:22 (NIV)*

When the heat is on, may we still praise Him. Pour yourself a steamy cup of coffee and take a moment to think about it!

---

[60] Psalm 92:12 (NIV)

24

My Cup Brims with Blessing

You prepare a table before me in the presence of my enemies;
You have anointed my head with oil;
My cup overflows.

Psalm 23:5 (NASB)

O f special interest is the phrase "My cup overflows". If you thumb through *The Cambridge Dictionary* to the verb 'overflow' you will discover the meaning:

When a liquid overflows, it flows over the edges of a container
etc. because there is too much of it.

The Hebrew word used in our verse suggests the idea of 'saturation'. The King James Version's wording is "my cup runneth over". Another translation puts it, "...my cup brims with blessing."[61] In the context of this verse and chapter, it speaks about God's provisions and blessings. When the "LORD is my shepherd"[62], "my cup runs over" in superabundance.

This psalm made sense to the Jews because when they received a guest, they would intentionally overfill the cup and allow it to run over and by doing this, the guest would know that they were welcome to stay as long as they wanted. The psalmist says that God has prepared the table for him (and us), He has anointed us with oil (representative of the Holy Spirit), and He has provided all that we will ever need, even in our times of need. Our cup is not half empty – it is overflowing. In John 10, the chapter about the Good Shepherd, Jesus said:

"I have come that they may have life, and have it to the full."

John 10:10 (NIV)

---

[61] MSG
[62] Psalm 23:1 (NKJV)

The life He gives us is *perisson*, meaning 'to have a surplus', 'superabundance', 'till it overflows'.

How much time do we spend in prayer thanking God for all that He has provided? In Christ we can have overflowing joy, overflowing love and overflowing peace.

> *God is able to make all grace abound toward you; that ye, always having all sufficiency in all things, may abound to every good work.*
>
> *2 Corinthians 9:8 (KJV)*

This was Paul's way of saying that our cup "runneth over". The Greek word translated "abound" in this passage means 'over and above', or in other words, 'running over'.

My cup runs over because He "is able to do far more abundantly beyond all that we ask or think, according to the power that works within us"[63]. Ephesians 1:3 says all believers already have "every spiritual blessing in the heavenly places"[64]. 2 Peter 1:3 says God has given His children "all things necessary for life and godliness"[65]. The Psalmist says, "He daily loadeth us with benefits,"[66] and, "Bless the Lord, O my soul, and forget not all His benefits: who forgives all your iniquities, who heals all your diseases, who redeems your life from destruction, who crowns you with lovingkindness and tender mercies, who satisfies your mouth with good things, so that your youth is renewed like the eagle's."[67]

In the Garden of Gethsemane, on the night before he was crucified, Jesus prayed and asked, "God, if you wish, take this cup from me," the cup that represented suffering and pain. But through his faithfulness, Christ has turned that cup of suffering into a cup of blessing, which now overflows for each and every one of us.

It's been said, "If you pause to think, you'll have cause to thank." Let's thank God that our cups brim with blessings.

---

[63] Ephesians 3:20 (NASB)
[64] ESV
[65] NET
[66] Psalm 68:19 (KJV)
[67] Psalm 103:2-5 (NKJV)

25

Biblical Blessedness

Blessed is the man
Who walks not in the counsel of the ungodly,
Nor stands in the path of sinners,
Nor sits in the seat of the scornful;
But his delight is in the law of the LORD,
And in His law he meditates day and night.

Psalm 1:1-2 (NKJV)

The Psalm begins with the word "blessed". In Hebrew the word is actually a plural, which denotes either a multiplicity of blessings or an intensification of them and literally means, 'Oh, the blessednesses (or the blessings).'

Notice the words "walks not ... nor stands ... nor sits". There is a way he will *not* walk, a path he will *not* stand in, and a seat he will *not* sit in.

He does not walks in the counsel of the ungodly. The word "ungodly" in Hebrew has the root idea of 'to be loose or unstable'. It means to be loose with morals. It also means loose from God, without Him as an anchor or controlling device. It refers to those who are controlled by their own desires, emotions and flesh rather than by God. We are to avoid counsel from those who do not have God as an anchor. Many fail at this point. They do not even consider if counsel is godly or ungodly. The righteous person knows where to find godly counsel:

Your testimonies also are my delight and my counselors.

Psalm 119:24 (AMPC)

God's Word is always the best counsellor, and godly counsellors will always bring forth the truth of God's Word. Paul tells us:

See then that ye walk circumspectly, not as fools, but as wise.

Ephesians 5:15 (KJV)

He does not stand in the path of sinners. Standing means something different than walking. To walk is to keep moving but to stand is to park yourself in a path. It's to stop and engage. Standing is a way of positioning yourself. The danger is that if a person listens to the world's counsel and its perspectives and imbibes the advice of the media, he/she will eventually get comfortable in the realm of sinful things, ungodly ways of thinking and living, and casually "stand in the way of sinners" rather than standing firm in the faith.[68] Remember that the path of sinners moves in the opposite direction from your destination! Don't dally in the path of temptation.

He does not sit in the seat of the scornful. To sit means to make yourself fully at home with a lifestyle. We are to avoid the seat of the scornful. That's from a word that means 'to deride, mock'. It refers to those who make what is good and holy the object of their ridicule. In the Book of Proverbs "the scorners" appear as a class of defiant and cynical freethinkers, in contrast and antagonism to "the wise". The root-principle of their character is a spirit of proud self-sufficiency and a contemptuous disregard for God and His ways, a cynic who mocks everything in a show of superiority. When you sit with the scoffers, it may not be long until a permanent chair is reserved for you.

Some see in the "walk", "stand," and "sit" imagery three degrees of departure from God and conformity to world. Check it out in the Amplified Bible:

> *Blessed (happy, fortunate, prosperous, and enviable) is the man who walks and lives not in the counsel of the ungodly [following their advice, their plans and purposes], nor stands [submissive and inactive] in the path where sinners walk, nor sits down [to relax and rest] where the scornful [and the mockers] gather.*
>
> *Psalm 1:1-2 (AMPC)*

The great lesson to be learned is to vigilantly walk closely with the Lord in the path of righteousness. May the Lord bless you on your journey.

---

68 See 1 Corinthians 16:13

26

The True Version of Reality

Now when the attendant of the man of God had risen early and gone out, behold, an army with horses and chariots was circling the city. And his servant said to him, "Alas, my master! What shall we do?" So he answered, "Do not fear, for those who are with us are more than those who are with them." Then Elisha prayed and said, "O LORD, I pray, open his eyes that he may see." And the LORD opened the servant's eyes and he saw; and behold, the mountain was full of horses and chariots of fire all around Elisha.

2 Kings 6:15-17 (NASB)

The Blind Men and the Elephant is a famous story which tells of six blind sojourners who came across different parts of an elephant in their life journeys. In turn, each blind man created his own version of reality from that limited experience and perspective. The first man reached out and touched the elephant grabbing the elephant's tail. "Aha," he exclaimed, "the elephant is like a big rope." The next man felt a massive elephant leg. "The elephant is like a large log or tree." He was sure of this. The third blind man felt the elephant's side, whereupon he pronounced that, "The elephant is really a big wall." Next, another of the blind men reached out and took hold of one of the elephant's ears. "Oh, the elephant is like a big fan." The fifth blind man put out his hand as the elephant raised his trunk. "It is obvious the elephant is like a huge snake." The final man encountered a tusk. He concluded, "I understand the true nature of the elephant is this: he is a sword."

None had seen the full elephantine picture. This was the problem which confronted the attendant of Elisha in 2 Kings 6. He was looking at his situation from the wrong vantage point. How often are we guilty of the same thing? In our modern parlance we probably have said, "Alas ... what shall I do?" We may not confront an armed barbarian horde in

126

our front yard waiting to harm us, but we all know what it's like to be suddenly confronted with problems beyond our control. And we all can relate to the servant's panic in the crisis. There are times when troubling situations come our way during the course of our lives. When this happens, we tend to only look at what we can see. However, there is far more to the picture than what these mortal eyes can behold. Elisha prayed and said, "O LORD, I pray, open his eyes that he may see." God answered and he saw the fuller picture, the horses and chariots of fire all around Elisha. He was actually seeing an angelic army of protection.

This reminds us to get our eyes off our circumstances and place them squarely upon the Lord. Look at things, not from a faulty human perspective, but from the perspective of God. His Word assures us:

> *The angel of the LORD encamps around those who fear Him, and delivers them.*
>
> *Psalm 34:7 (ESV)*

May the Lord open our eyes that we may see the true version of reality. God is all-sufficient and able to deal with any problem you have, no matter how big it is to you. A woman approached the well-known Bible teacher G. Campbell Morgan and asked, "Dr Morgan, do you think we should pray about little things, or just about big problems?" He straightened up and in his formal British manner said, "Madam, can you think of anything in your life that is big to God?" Our God is omniscient and omnipotent. He spoke the universe into existence. He is sovereign. Nothing is too difficult for Him.

27

Effective by Being Silent

The righteous choose their friends carefully,
but the way of the wicked leads them astray.

Proverbs 12:26 (NIV)

We are known by the company we keep, and the people with whom we choose to surround ourselves invariably have a strong influence on our beliefs and actions. That's why the Bible encourages us to choose our company carefully. Wise Christian friends will build us up, help us grow spiritually and bring wisdom. A bad friend will encourage ungodly traits, be a negative influence and lead us astray.

As iron sharpens iron,
so a friend sharpens a friend.

Proverbs 27:17 (NLT)

There is mutual benefit in the rubbing of two iron blades together; the edges become sharper, making the knives more efficient in their task to cut and slice. Two solid Christian friends can also have the same type of positive effect on one another by sharing their own personal walks in the Lord with mutual edification. We see this Scripture exemplified in the lives of David and Jonathan, Ruth and Naomi, and Paul and Timothy. Do you have other 'irons' in your life who can help in sharpening you?

We truly become more effective by being selective in our choice of friends.

Walk with the wise and become wise;
associate with fools and get in trouble.

Proverbs 13:20 (NLT)

Or as The Message Bible states:

Become wise by walking with the wise;
hang out with fools and watch your life fall to pieces.

Proverbs 13:20 (MSG)

Preferring the wise as friends does not imply that you stop evangelising the lost. Jesus' call for you to stay in the world and be his witness to all still applies. God asks us to be a friend to many, extend kindness and help to those around us – this scripture isn't telling us to be exclusive with our love, it's telling us to be wise with whom we let influence our path in life.

The alternative to walking with the wise is surrounding oneself with fools, and Proverbs 13:20 warns us that those who do that will "suffer harm"[69]. Here, the harm in view is harm to the entire person. In the New Testament Paul warns us:

Don't link up with those who will pollute you.

2 Corinthians 6:14 (MSG)

In other words, break up with bad company.

Do not be misled: "Bad company corrupts good character."

1 Corinthians 15:33 (NIV)

Hebrews 10 encourages us:

And let us consider how we may spur one another on toward
love and good deeds.

Hebrews 10:24 (NIV)

Forge friendships with your brothers and sisters in Christ and encourage one another as fellow labourers. Studies say you become like the five people closest to you. Who are the good influencers in our lives?

[69] ESV

28

That's Not All Folks!

For to me, to live is Christ and to die is gain... having the desire to depart and be with Christ, for that is very much better.

Philippians 1:21-23 (NASB)

Although you may have never seen Mel Blanc's face, you've probably heard his voice. He voiced hundreds of classic cartoon characters including Bugs Bunny, Porky Pig, Daffy Duck, Sylvester the Cat and other Warner Bros. creations. The repertoire of this versatile voice actor includes Bugs' catchy cue: "What's up, doc?" and Tweety Pie, the devious canary known for the song *I Tawt I Taw a Puddy Tat*. Blanc's first major character was Porky Pig, the shy stammerer known for his signature line, "Th-th-th-that's all, folks!" Viewers always knew they had reached the end of the cartoon when they heard Porky Pig say, "That's all, folks!" This line became the catchphrase on the banner shown at the end of Looney Tunes cartoons. When Blanc was buried in the Hollywood Forever cemetery, he made this catchphrase his own final farewell. The epitaph on his tombstone reads, "That's All, Folks."

But that's *not* all, folks! Death is not the end. There is more to the story! In today's reading we see the entire substance of Paul's life and what he looked to beyond this life: to be with Christ. Paul knew that death is not a defeat to the Christian but is merely a graduation to glory, a 'net gain' in accounting terms. In another passage brimming with comfort, Paul affirms that "to be absent from the body" is in reality "to be at home with the Lord"[70].

John Newton was a great preacher and hymn-writer known for the words of *Amazing Grace*. Two years before his death, in 1807, he was so weak that he could hardly stand in his pulpit; someone had to support him as he preached. Shortly before he died, when he was confined to his

---

[70] 2 Corinthians 5:8 (NASB)

room and unable to move, he told a friend, "I am like a person going on a journey in a stagecoach, who expects its arrival every hour and is frequently looking out of the window for it – I am packed and sealed, and ready for the post."

Jesus said to Martha:

> *"I am the resurrection and the life. The one who believes in me will live, even though they die; and whoever lives and believes in me will never die. Do you believe this?"*
>
> *John 11:25-26 (NIV)*

Do *you* believe this? "That's all, folks" or "that's *not* all, folks"?

29

Your Inner Orchard

But what happens when we live God's way? He brings gifts into our lives, much the same way that fruit appears in an orchard – things like affection for others, exuberance about life, serenity. We develop a willingness to stick with things, a sense of compassion in the heart, and a conviction that a basic holiness permeates things and people. We find ourselves involved in loyal commitments, not needing to force our way in life, able to marshal and direct our energies wisely.

Galatians 5:22-23 (MSG)

County Armagh is the smallest county in Northern Ireland, at 1,254 km². It is known as the Orchard County because of the number of apple orchards. Their produce is mainly apples of the Bramley variety. It is said that St Patrick planted the first apple tree in Armagh but the Bramley was introduced to the county in 1884 and the apple industry quickly became a major employer in the county. The orchards of County Armagh produce more than forty thousand tonnes of Bramley apples annually. Fruit is important business in that county but also in the life of the Christian.

Having taught at length on the fruit of the Spirit on many occasions, it is easy to rattle off the different qualities or fruit which should be evident in our lives:

The fruit of the Spirit is love, joy, peace, longsuffering, kindness, goodness, faithfulness, gentleness, self-control.

Galatians 5:22-23 (NKJV)

That is why I appreciate reading another translation which takes me out of my comfort zone and causes me to pause and ponder afresh. Today's reading is taken from the Message Bible.

What happens when we live God's way? Here is the list:

- affection for others;

- exuberance about life;
- serenity;
- a willingness to stick with things;
- a sense of compassion in the heart;
- a conviction that a basic holiness permeates things and people;
- involvement in loyal commitments;
- not needing to force our way in life;
- able to marshal and direct our energies wisely.

Yield to the Holy Spirit and let the harvest come to fruition in your inner orchard. May our fruit be delightful to the core and visible and appealing to others. As Paul said:

> *We pray that you'll live well for the Master, making Him proud of you as you work hard in His orchard.*
>
> Colossians 1:10 (MSG)

30

The Misunderstood Magpie

He was despised and rejected by mankind,
a man of suffering, and familiar with pain.

Isaiah 53:3 (NIV)

Their numbers in Britain and Ireland have quadrupled in the last thirty-five years. They are non-migratory, and it's rare for one to ever travel more than ten kilometres from where it was hatched. In bright sunlight they are the most exquisitely beautiful birds, with that lovely long tail and iridescence. However, magpies are viewed as nefarious creatures and their stereotype is far from favourable. Magpies have always been surrounded by superstition, and there are many versions of the poem that begins, "One for sorrow, two for joy..." There was an old rural tradition of raising one's hat to a magpie; now that few people wear hats, the tradition has largely died out. Magpies are also surrounded by rumours of kleptomania, avidly collecting shiny objects to adorn their nests. In 1815, two French playwrights penned a historical melodrama in which a servant is sentenced to death for stealing silverware from her master, when the real thief is his pet magpie. Moved by the Parisian urban myth, Gioachino Rossini set his opera *La Gazza Ladra* to the same story. This effectively nailed the magpie's character to the gibbet of popular opinion. According to latest scientific research, however, the reality is that magpies are not thieves, merely inquisitive. As members of the Corvidae family, they are often associated with a long history of fear and loathing and a group of them is called 'a murder of magpies'. Many people fear them simply because of their black feathers, which associates them with death. Again, research proves that magpies are actually very social and caring creatures, and also among the smartest animals on the planet. Magpies have been shown to possess the intellectual prowess necessary to recognise themselves in a mirror – a feat that, until now, has only been seen in humans, apes, elephants and dolphins.

Nobody likes to be misunderstood. As painful as it may be if you are misunderstood, remember that you are in good company. David was misunderstood by his older brother as being proud and deceitful when he inquired about the possibility of confronting and killing the giant Goliath.[71] Hannah was misunderstood by the High Priest Eli as being a drunken woman when she fervently but silently prayed to God for the blessing of a child.[72] Jesus was misunderstood probably more than any other person.

> *Is this not the carpenter, the son of Mary, and the brother of James and Joses and Judas and Simon? ... And they were [deeply] offended by Him...*
>
> *Mark 6:3 (AMP)*

> *He came to His own, and His own did not receive Him.*
>
> *John 1:11 (NKJV)*

One of the prophecies about the Messiah foretold that He would be "despised and rejected by men"[73]. One thing we know for sure, Jesus did not contribute to their wrong perceptions. Those who entertained these wrong ideas did so because of their own issues. Their tainted filters led to wrong imaginations about who He was and why He was doing what He was doing.

If you are one that has been misunderstood, then take heart. Jesus understands how you feel.

> *Who, when he was reviled, reviled not again; when he suffered, he threatened not; but committed himself to him that judgeth righteously.*
>
> *1 Peter 2:23 (KJV)*

He could have fought back, proving his innocence. He could have called for twelve legions of angels to come to his rescue at any moment. But instead He remained misunderstood, even to death, because He trusted His Father.

Feeling misunderstood? Look to the cross. For our part, let's not jump to conclusions about others. Avoid acting solely on assumptions absent

---

[71] See 1 Samuel 17:26-28
[72] See 1 Samuel 1:13
[73] Isaiah 53:3 (AMP)

of facts and based only on appearances or our preconceived notions. Let's do our best to be understanding.

31

Let the Redeemed of the Lord Say So

Oh give thanks to the LORD, for He is good,
For His lovingkindness is everlasting.
Let the redeemed of the LORD say so,
Whom He has redeemed from the hand of the adversary.

Psalm 107:1-2 (NASB)

We are called "the redeemed of the Lord". When we look at our English word "redeemed", the first three letters say it all: *red*. Red reminds us of the precious blood shed for our redemption. There are a number of different words used in the original Greek which are translated into English as "redeemed", each giving us another nuance of its meaning. Check out the following:

The first is *agorazo*. The noun *agora* is Greek for a marketplace, a wide, open public space. The English word 'agoraphobia' is derived from it, meaning a fear of open spaces. The verb *agorazo* translated as "redeemed" literally means 'to do business in the marketplace', in other words, to buy, to purchase, or to acquire ownership by payment of a price. We know the purchase price in our case is the blood of God's own Son.

For ye are bought with a price...

1 Corinthians 6:20 (KJV)

...you were not redeemed with corruptible things, like silver or gold, from your aimless conduct received by tradition from your fathers, but with the precious blood of Christ, as of a lamb without blemish and without spot. He indeed was foreordained before the foundation of the world, but was manifest in these last times for you .

1 Peter 1:18-20 (NKJV)

The second is *exagorazo*. Look familiar? It is the same word as above with *ex* on the front of it. That means it is a strengthened form of *agorazo. Ex* means 'out of', think of exit, way out. We have been redeemed out of something, into something. Paul said:

> ...*Who hath delivered us from the power of darkness, and hath translated us into the kingdom of his dear Son:*
> *In whom we have redemption through his blood, even the forgiveness of sins...*
>
> *Colossians 1:13-14 (KJV)*

The third word is *lutroo.* The root of *lutroo, luo,* means 'to loosen, unbind, or untie, to set at liberty'. It was the price of release, the substitution of money for a slave in order to set him free. The underlying purpose behind Christ's redemptive work is freedom to fulfil our potential.

> ...*Who gave Himself for us, that He might redeem us from all iniquity, and purify unto Himself a peculiar people, zealous of good works.*
>
> *Titus 2:14 (KJV)*

Let's give thanks to the Lord, for He is good, for His lovingkindness is everlasting. Let the redeemed of the Lord say so, whom He has redeemed from the hand of the adversary.

August

August

1

Ollie the Owl

First of all, then, I urge that supplications, prayers, intercessions, and thanksgivings be made for all people, for kings and all who are in high positions, that we may lead a peaceful and quiet life, godly and dignified in every way.

1 Timothy 2:1-2 (ESV)

When my children were younger, one of their favourite stories was *Ollie the Owl Learns to Fly*. It was a pop-up book and had its own mobile owl which could fly off at the end of the story creating lots of excitement. In real life owls are intriguing creatures, especially when you see them rotating their heads 270 degrees! But I came across a few facts which were not so appealing. Apparently, they eat their prey whole and then barf up the carcass. They sometimes eat other owls too! Great horned owls are actually the chief predation threat to the smaller barred owl. In turn, barred owls will eat even smaller owls.

Interestingly, a group of owls is called a 'parliament'. This is said to have originated because they have long been considered to be of a wise disposition. Do you remember the following English nursery rhyme:

A wise old owl lived in an oak.
The more he saw the less he spoke.
The less he spoke the more he heard.
Why can't we all be like that wise old bird?

The word 'parliament' actually comes from the French word *parler* meaning 'to speak'. Public debate, exchanging arguments and even political disputes governed by clearly defined rules are the core business of any parliament. Parliament has the opportunity to speak on many issues and it is our responsibility to pray that they do so with wisdom. The Bible tells us to pray for "all who are in high positions".

Pray for policy issues abroad; pray also for domestic policy issues, and for responsibilities towards those in education, health, police, the armed forces, social and welfare services. Pray for them to handle issues of terrorism, its threat and its causes, with great wisdom. Political decisions affect key biblical issues like justice for the poor, the moral character of the nation and freedom to proclaim the gospel message. Pray for effective Christian presence and influence in political debate, and for laws and policies which reflect God's word and wisdom.

Let us do our part so that we can "lead a peaceful and quiet life, godly and dignified in every way".

2

Bringing a Brolly

*And without faith it is impossible to please God, because
anyone who comes to him must believe that He exists and that
He rewards those who earnestly seek Him.*

Hebrews 11:6 (NIV)

*L*iving in Northern Ireland, I don't venture far without my umbrella. Unless you like the wet dog look, a basic brolly is essential. Just to brighten up a dull rainy day, my daughter has one of those umbrellas which changes colour when wet. The raindrops suddenly turn into a rainbow of colour. As it dries, the colours fade to black – awaiting its next task when the clouds bring rain again.

I remember hearing a story about a drought which affected a small community of farmers. Rain was important to keep their crops healthy and sustain their way of life. As the problem became more acute, the local pastor called a special service to pray for rain. Many people came to the service to pray and as the pastor looked out over the crowd he was encouraged. However, the thing that inspired him most was a little girl sitting in the front pew, holding a bright red umbrella. Everyone had come to pray for rain, but only the little girl believed enough to bring an umbrella. All came to pray for rain, but the little girl had come expecting God to answer.

Prayer is asking for rain. Faith is carrying an umbrella. In Hebrews 11 we are told:

*And without faith it is impossible to please God, because
anyone who comes to him must believe that He exists and that
He rewards those who earnestly seek Him.*

Hebrews 11:6 (NIV)

He rewards those who earnestly seek Him. Jesus said:

> *"Therefore I tell you, whatever you ask for in prayer, believe that you have received it, and it will be yours."*
>
> *Mark 11:24 (NIV)*

Believe that you have received it. In His sermon on the mount, Jesus said:

> *"Ask and it will be given to you; seek and you will find; knock and the door will be opened to you. For everyone who asks receives; he who seek finds; and to him who knocks, the door will be opened."*
>
> *Matthew 7:7-8 (NIV)*

Do you expect God to answer your prayers? Are you simply turning to pray at the prayer meeting or are you coming to see God's answer?

3

Standing on the Surelys of God

And the LORD said, I have surely seen the affliction of my people which are in Egypt, and have heard their cry by reason of their taskmasters; for I know their sorrows.

Exodus 3:7 (KJV)

I love the word 'surely'. It's not maybe or perhaps or possibly. It speaks of certainty and exudes confidence. There are many examples in the Bible, such as:

Surely goodness and mercy shall follow me all the days of my life…

Psalm 23:6 (ESV)

Surely He will save you from the fowler's snare and from the deadly pestilence.

Psalm 91:3 (NIV)

Surely He has borne our griefs and carried our sorrows.

Isaiah 53:4 (NKJV)

"And surely I am with you always, to the very end of the age."

Matthew 28:20 (NIV)

Surely I come quickly. Amen. Even so, come, Lord Jesus.

Revelation 22:20 (KJV)

But today let us stand on the "surely" of Exodus 3:7. Isn't it reassuring when God says, "I have surely seen the affliction of my people"? God can see every affliction of His people even when it is hidden from man. Some people are adept at hiding the inner conflicts from others. Some can masterfully mask their true struggles and camouflage or conceal their condition. But the Lord knows for sure. The Lord informed Moses that He had "seen" their affliction and "heard" their cries, and He "knew" their sorrows. It is the same with us.

- God has seen your affliction.
- God has heard your cry.
- God knows your sorrows.

Whatever pain or suffering or challenges we go through in life, God sees, hears and knows about them. He is indeed touched with the feeling of our infirmities and afflictions and sorrows.[74]

Maybe you, or someone you know, are in a season of feeling like God is deaf to your cries, blind to your circumstances or unwilling to listen. Take a moment to read Hagar's story in Genesis 16. Hagar found herself in dire straits right in the middle of the wilderness. Help from man was nowhere to be found. Nonetheless, God saw her and – in His great mercy and love – manifested Himself unto her and saved her life. Verse 11 holds the key words:

"...the Lord has heard your cry of distress."

Genesis 16:11 (GNB)

In verse 13 Hagar declares:

"You are the God who sees me."

Genesis 16:13 (NIV)

What we witness in this story and in Exodus 3 is a God who is fully engaged with the plight of the oppressed, a God who is moved by their cries, and a God who responds with action. Today remember that God surely sees, God surely hears and God surely knows.

---

[74] See Hebrews 4:15

4

Fun With Siri

He who dwells in the shelter of the Most High
will abide in the shadow of the Almighty.
I will say to the LORD, "My refuge and my fortress,
my God, in whom I trust."

Psalm 91:1-2 (ESV)

Siri, the digital voice built into Apple's iOS devices, is very obviously not human yet it still cleverly answers multiple questions. Siri regularly elicits some humour, and it can be a great way to have a giggle.

Ask Siri, "What are you wearing?"

Siri: "Aluminosilicate silicate glass and steel, nice huh?"

Ask Siri, "Why did the chicken cross the road?"

Siri answers, "I am not perspicacious about the peregrinations of poultry."

One of the popular questions to ask Siri is, "How much wood would a woodchuck chuck if a woodchuck could chuck wood?"

Siri seems less than amused by this riddle and offers a number of responses. "A so-called woodchuck (correctly speaking, a groundhog) would chuck – that is, throw – as much as the woodchuck in question was physically able to chuck, if woodchucks in general had the capability and presumably, the motivation, to chuck wood."

Sometimes Siri answers, "Don't you have anything better to do?"

The woodchuck is indeed a complex character who lives underground and his apartment has both front doors and back doors. If the fox snoops in one door, he can exit the other. Burrows will have 'spy holes', or smaller, more concealed entrances, out of which the woodchuck can look across its home range or in an emergency rapidly escape from one of its multiple exits. The living quarters are about six feet beneath the surface and wind around for about eight to sixty-six feet (two to twenty metres).

The creature spends a lot of its time digging, as you can imagine! And it's all for security.

We all face different fears and challenges on a daily basis. There may be even times when fear influences us to such an extent that it impacts the decisions we make. Psalm 91 gives us the assurance that we have a divine promise of security as a child of God. In some Bible translations, it is subtitled "The Security Of The One Who Trusts In The Lord". In verse 1, God is called the "Most High" and the "Almighty". When we acknowledge Him as the Most High and call on Him as the Almighty and know Him as "my God" like the Psalmist in verse 2, we can abide in the assurance of safety and security. As children of God, we have a secret place where nothing and no-one can cause us lasting pain. When we are walking close to God and find our shelter with Him, we can rest under His divine wing of protection.

5

Do It Heartily

Whatever you do, work heartily, as for the Lord and not for men...

Colossians 3:23 (ESV)

*I*f you have watched Walt Disney's 1937 animated film *Snow White and the Seven Dwarfs* you will be familiar with the lyrics, "Hi ho, hi ho, it's off to work we go!" It is sung by the group of seven dwarfs as they work at a mine with diamonds and rubies and is one of the best-known songs in the film. A modern parody version of the song is, "I owe, I owe, so off to work I go!"

Work is a huge part of each of our lives. Whether you are out in the workforce, or you are a student at school, or you are a mother at home, you spend a significant amount of your time working. What is your attitude to work? Have a look at Colossians 3:23:

"Whatever you do..." "Whatever" includes any and all contexts. It includes doing the dishes or picking up toys for the thousandth time. It includes folding countless loads of laundry every week and it includes vacuuming, grocery shopping and doing any mundane task.

"...work heartily..." Christians are to work "heartily", from the Greek phrase *ek psyches*, meaning 'from the soul'. This implies the idea of enthusiasm and passion. Demonstrating a good work attitude makes a tremendous difference in your personal life and in your influence on others.

Whatever your hand finds to do, do it with all your might...

Ecclesiastes 9:10 (AMPC)

"...as for the Lord..." Our true employer is God. This one principle will revolutionise your attitude at work. See your job as service to Him – not simply to your employer. This applies not merely to pastors and missionaries; it is a truth for bankers, baristas, lawyers, doctors, construction workers, etc.

Don't just do what you have to do to get by, but work heartily, as Christ's servants doing what God wants you to do. And work with a smile on your face, always keeping in mind that no matter who happens to be giving the orders, you're really serving God. Good work will get you good pay from the Master...

Ephesians 6:6-8 (MSG)

Whatever your task today, work heartily and remember whom you are really serving.

6

Go With the Grain

*...all the days ordained for me were written in your book
before one of them came to be.*

Psalm 139:16 (NIV)

*M*y husband is a carpenter/joiner and has the ability to make a piece of wood become something useful and beautiful. When choosing floors and decor for our home I learned that wood comes in many varieties, each with its own characteristics and appeal. Colour, grain and texture can vary dramatically. I also observed that in woodworking it is important to be aware of the grain of the wood. If you go against the grain you can scar the wood and upset its natural appearance. When you use a sanding block or an electric sander, you want to make smooth passes in the direction of the grain of the wood.

In woodworking it is important to go with the grain; so it is with God's design for our lives. Going against the grain is messy and can scar us. So many of us twist ourselves up in knots trying desperately to be something or someone else. The Bible says that we must individually "run with patience the particular race that God has set before us"[75]. Don't be envious of the runner in the lane next to you; just focus on finishing your race. Instead of wishing you were someone else, thank God for making you the person you are. Your shape was sovereignly determined by God for His purpose, so you shouldn't resent it or reject it. You are custom-designed for your calling. You are fearfully and wonderfully made.[76]

All the days ordained for me were written in your book before one of them came to be.

Psalm 139:16 (NIV)

So live out God's plans and show your true colours.

---

[75] Hebrews 12:1 (TLB)
[76] See Psalm 139:14

It's time to peel off the layers of expectation and pressure that come from opinionated people around us. Refuse to compete or compare yourself with someone else. God did not make you a carbon-copy.

> *"For I know the plans I have for you,"* declares the LORD, *"plans to prosper you and not to harm you, plans to give you hope and a future."*
>
> *Jeremiah 29:11 (NIV)*

The challenge for us is to remind ourselves that our job in life is to be the person God made us to be and to go with the grain. Celebrate your uniqueness.

> *Christ has given each of us special abilities – whatever He wants us to have out of his rich storehouse of gifts.*
>
> *Ephesians 4:7 (TLB)*

Surround yourself with people who are not intimidated by your assignment, who are comfortable with their own assignment, and who can help you run your race. When you are comfortable with who God has made you to be and what He has called you to do, you are in position to allow God to use your uniqueness for His glory and add lustre to the lives of others. When you have this mindset, you'll love and appreciate everyone in your life, for each one adds his or her own unique colour and perspective.

7

Please, Sir, I Want Some More

If you then, who are evil, know how to give good gifts to your children, how much more will your Father who is in heaven give good things to those who ask him!

Matthew 7:11 (ESV)

The words, "Please, sir, I want some more," may ring a bell. Nine-year-old Oliver Twist was a resident in the parish workhouse where the boys were "issued three meals of thin gruel a day, with an onion twice a week, and half a roll on Sundays". Under this regimen which reduced the boys to living skeletons, Oliver and his companions became the victims of slow starvation. Eventually they held a council among themselves and resolved to choose by lot one of their number to ask the overseer for more gruel. The outcome of the lottery fell on Oliver Twist. In the book we are told:

> *He rose from the table; and advancing to the master, basin and spoon in hand, said: somewhat alarmed at his own temerity:*
> *"Please, sir, I want some more."*
> *The master was a fat, healthy man; but he turned very pale. He gazed in stupefied astonishment on the small rebel for some seconds, and then clung for support to the copper. The assistants were paralysed with wonder; the boys with fear.*
> *"What!" said the master at length, in a faint voice.*
> *"Please, sir," replied Oliver, "I want some more."*
> *The master aimed a blow at Oliver's head with the ladle; pinioned him in his arms; and shrieked aloud...*[77]

By contrast we read in Matthew 7:11 concerning God:

---

[77] Charles Dickens; *Oliver Twist*

"If you, then, though you are evil, know how to give good gifts to your children, how much more will your Father in heaven give good gifts to those who ask him!"

Matthew 7:11 (NIV)

Notice the words "how much more". Rather than berate us for asking, He blesses us and loves to give good gifts. James said:

Every good gift and every perfect gift is from above, coming down from the Father of lights with whom there is no variation or shadow due to change.

James 1:17 (ESV)

He gives good things. The only requirement on our part is to ask. Note the final phrase in Matthew 7:11, "to those who ask Him". How much blessing we forfeit because we do not ask! While God knows our needs before we ask and is intimately concerned, we are, nevertheless, to take our needs and those of others to God's throne of grace in prayer. We can confidently approach the throne of grace to receive mercy and find grace whenever we need help.

The little orphan boy in Charles Dickens' classic, *Oliver Twist,* dared to pose the outrageous request for a second helping. How about you? Seconds and thirds and endless helpings of his truth and grace await us every time we pray. Oh, that God would make us insatiable in wanting the more that He longs to provide.

8

Where's Wally?

Then the man and his wife heard the sound of the LORD God
as he was walking in the garden in the cool of the day, and
they hid from the LORD God among the trees of the garden.
But the LORD God called to the man, "Where are you?"

Genesis 3:8-9 (NIV)

The objective of each *Where's Wally?* book (or *Where's Waldo?* in the USA) is simple: you comb through a plethora of people to locate the bespectacled Wally, who's always wearing his red and white striped jumper. Spotting the elusive Wally is an exercise in patience and frustration. You're looking through what seems like a swarm of people wearing red and white, sometimes thinking you found him only to be mistaken for the wrong person, a beach towel or an umbrella.

Scientists reveal how to find the character in the shortest time possible. A computer scientist has devised a strategy using machine learning and algorithms to find him speedily. Apparently, Wally is rarely located in the top left-hand corner, or along the edges. He is also never found on the bottom of the right-hand page.

While you're busy frantically searching for him, you can't always appreciate just how impressive the level of detail is on each page. Every scene took Handford, the artist, around eight weeks to finish. But despite the care that goes into every inch of the page, the placement of Wally himself isn't exactly a science. "As I work my way through a picture, I add Wally when I come to what I feel is a good place to hide him," Handford said.

"Where are you?" is the first question asked by God in the Bible. Genesis 3:7-10 tells us of the efforts that Adam and Eve made to hide from God. Of course, no-one can hide from Him.[78] God knew exactly

---

[78] See Psalm 139:1-12; Proverbs 15:3; Jeremiah 23:24

where Adam and Eve were physically located. The question was for *their* benefit. He wasn't looking for a missing person when He asked Adam and Eve where they were hiding – He wanted them to understand the full ramifications of what they had done. Every question God asks is carefully crafted and specifically designed to lead to our self-reflection and, if necessary, self-correction and restoration.

"Where are you?" Are you dressed in fig leaves or garments of salvation? Just as He asked Adam and Eve, the Lord is asking you today. How are you going to answer Him? Are you walking right beside Him or are you hiding somewhere behind the 'bushes' of denial and blame-shifting?

9

History is His Story

For whatsoever things were written aforetime were written for our learning, that we through patience and comfort of the scriptures might have hope.

Romans 15:4 (KJV)

*M*any people believe that history is meaningless. In 1916 Henry Ford, the impresario of the mass automobile, stated sweepingly, "History is bunk." This old-fashioned term is derived from the Dutch *bunkum*, meaning 'rubbish' or 'nonsense'. On the other hand, Oliver Wendell Holmes, Jr., said, "When I want to understand what is happening today or try to decide what will happen tomorrow, I look back." He also observed, "A page of history is worth a volume of logic."[79] History helps us understand who we are by showing us where we have come from. This is even more true of the inspired history recorded in Scripture for our growth in godliness.

History is 'His story'. "In the beginning, God." So starts HIStory. In the Bible we are able to study the past events and purposes of God and man. We are able to 'go back in time', to explore and come to understand eras we never lived through ourselves. We are told explicitly in Romans 15:4 that these things were written for our learning. Interestingly the term 'history' is derived from an ancient Greek verb which means 'to know', according to the Oxford English Dictionary. Romans 15:4 contains a principle of great significance for the twentieth-century believer. Everything that was written in Scripture in days gone by was written for our learning. Not only did it serve the needs of its own day, but it is still relevant in the modern world. As Spurgeon put it:

Things written aforetime were written for our time.

---

[79] *Peter's Quotations;* Bantam Books, p.244

The Old Testament relates the story of God's history with his people from the very earliest times. It reveals God's power, faithfulness, and love. We can learn from the faith of God's people – and from their faithlessness as well. We can be inspired by their stories. The stories of Abraham, Jacob, Joseph, David, Job, etc. were written so that we might see how God worked in their lives, controlling their circumstances for their good and His glory. In the pages of Scripture, we find the teachings of endurance and encouragement.

As our verse says in another translation:

> For everything that was written in the past was written to teach us, so that through the endurance taught in the Scriptures and the encouragement they provide we might have hope.
>
> *Romans 15:4 (NIV)*

The end goal is to live in hope. Let us be thankful to God for the Scriptures, learn from them, apply their messages to our lives, develop endurance and be encouraged from the examples of the past.

10

Colour Within the Lines

Blessed is the one
whose transgressions are forgiven,
whose sins are covered.

Psalm 32:1 (NIV)

Colouring books – they're not just for kids anymore. I have noticed a resurgence lately of colouring books which are aimed at an adult audience. In a busy world, increasingly dominated by time spent in front of screens, grownups are turning to the soothing art of colouring in. These books, however, are not reminiscent of the freebie colouring sheets of animals and landscapes handed out at chain restaurants in our childhoods. These are intricately designed books, some created specifically to help you destress and focus the mind.

Why are grownups buying up a genre generally targeted at younger children? Does it work? Is it about nostalgia? Can we really find relief in colouring carefully in between the lines? The answer seems to be that colouring between the lines can be a therapeutic exercise. It bothered me as a child when someone sloppily coloured in a picture (especially if it was my book) without any reference to the lines. Adhering to boundaries is an important part of our development. Colouring outside the lines is messy.

God has established lines, marking out moral boundaries for individuals and societies. We live in a world which loves to tell us that lines don't matter. It is easy to see where people are colouring outside the lines these days in terms of biblical morality. Some people transgress boundaries in the name of self-expression. The boundaries set forth by our Creator were not to limit our self-expression, but to channel our own creativity in ways that lead to life and a deeper relationship to the One who made us and gave us our sense of worth. There is tremendous beauty and creativity to be discovered within the lines of submission to truth as revealed in Scripture. God's boundaries are not meant to curb our potential, but to protect and promote it.

In today's reading, we see the word "transgressions". The Hebrew word for "transgress" means 'to step across' or 'to go beyond a set boundary or limit'. It means 'to step over the line, to rebel against the authority of God'. A trespasser is someone who crosses a line or climbs a fence that he should not cross or climb. Our lives are best when lived within the confines and boundaries set by God's Word. Our lives are blessed when we live according to the Word, not the world. Let's keep within the lines.

11

A Black Hole

He put me in a black hole,
  buried me like a corpse in that dungeon.
I sat there in despair, my spirit draining away,
  my heart heavy, like lead.

Psalm 143:3-4 (MSG)

Albert Einstein first predicted black holes in 1916 with his general theory of relativity. The physicist John Wheeler is credited with coining the term 'black hole' which he first used in 1967. These black holes have given way to much scientific study in recent decades. NASA is presently using satellites and telescopes that are travelling in space to learn more about them.

As we read Psalm 143, we see that David was depressed. He was in a 'black hole'. How do you begin to get yourself out of a situation like this?

- *Remember the good things.* In this dark season of his soul, David remembered, considering the days of old when things were not so bad.

  I remember the days of long ago;
    I meditate on all your works
    and consider what your hands have done.

  Psalm 143:5 (NIV)

- *Keep worshipping.* Thankfully, the ache in David's soul did not drive him away from God. It drove him to God in prayer, praise and deep longing. Worship can be an oasis in difficult times. David says:

  I spread out my hands to you;
    I thirst for you like a parched land.

  Psalm 143:6 (NIV)

- *Cry out to God for help.* David prays:

LORD, hear my prayer...

Psalm 143:1 (NIV)

Answer me quickly, LORD...

Psalm 143:7 (NIV)

- *Listen for God's guidance.*

  Show me the way I should go,
  for to you I entrust my life.

Psalm 143:8 (NIV)

It is possible to escape from a black hole of despair. In Psalm 107 we are told, "Some sat in darkness, in utter darkness..."[80] We are told, "...they cried to the LORD in their trouble, and He saved them from their distress. He brought them out of darkness, the utter darkness."[81]

Your black hole may be invisible to those around you, but God sees the seriousness of your situation. He can bring you out of darkness and lift you from the pit of despair.[82]

---

[80] Psalm 107:10 (NIV)
[81] Psalm 107:10 (NIV)
[82] See Psalm 40:1-3

12

Forecourt Faux Pas

Wherefore do ye spend money for that which is not bread? and your labour for that which satisfieth not? hearken diligently unto me, and eat ye that which is good, and let your soul delight itself in fatness.

Isaiah 55:2 (KJV)

Apparently every three and a half minutes one UK motorist puts diesel in a petrol car or petrol in a diesel car. Do the maths and that's around 150,000 cases a year. It's an increasingly common forecourt faux-pas especially for two-car families which have one of each type of car and are in a rush for work or simply not thinking straight. You're far from alone if you find yourself in a predicament at the pump. The most common boo-boo is putting petrol in a diesel car. It's easier to do that because a petrol pump nozzle fits more easily into a diesel filler neck than the other way round. Sadly, a misfuelling misadventure can be costly and disrupt your journey.

In the journey of life man was not designed to "live by bread alone, but by every word that comes from the mouth of God"[83]. God designed the Bible to be a storehouse of nourishing soul food for His saints. Yet sadly too many of us feed our souls on the wrong fuel. In Isaiah 55 he addresses those who are thirsty.

"Is anyone thirsty? Come and drink..."

Isaiah 55:1 (TLB)

He invites us to fuel up and says in verse 2:

---

[83] Matthew 4:4 (ESV)

Why do you spend money for what is not bread, and your wages for what does not satisfy? Listen carefully to Me, and eat what is good, and delight yourself in abundance.

Isaiah 55:2 (NASB)

The prosperity of our souls depends on our spiritual food choices. If we tank up only on the fare that is offered every night on multiple media sources, we should not be surprised if we are spiritually sluggish and unsatisfied. Isaiah says, "...eat what is good, and you will delight in the richest of fare."[84]

Perhaps you haven't yet topped up with the wrong fuel, but maybe you have knowingly driven with the fuel light on. You think, "What's the big deal? My car has a reserve of fuel built in and I don't need to panic for a number of miles." However, experts tell us that driving our cars with only a small amount of fuel in the tank is not a good idea as we will be dragging sediment through our fuel system. Spiritually let us keep topped up with God's Word, the right fuel, and gain strength and direction for the journey ahead.

...for then you shall make your way prosperous, and then you shall have good success.

Joshua 1:8 (WEB)

---

[84] Isaiah 55:2 (NIV)

13

Little and Wise

There be four things which are little upon the earth, but they are exceeding wise:
The ants are a people not strong, yet they prepare their meat in the summer;
The conies are but a feeble folk, yet make they their houses in the rocks;
The locusts have no king, yet go they forth all of them by bands;
The spider taketh hold with her hands, and is in kings' palaces.

Proverbs 30:24-28 (KJV)

Felix was born in the early third century in Nola, near Naples, in present day Italy. The reason I know of him is because of a spider. Felix was running from Roman soldiers and found an abandoned shack to hide in. A spider spun a web over the entrance, hiding him from discovery. The pursuers arrived and wondered if he was hiding there, but on seeing the unbroken and unmangled piece of art, thought it impossible for him to have entered without dismantling the web. And so they went on their way.

Proverbs lists four "little" things that are "exceeding wise": ants, conies, locusts and spiders. Each has a message for us. The message of the ant in Proverbs 30:25 is to prepare for your eternal future. Don't just live for the now. The message of the conies in Proverbs 30:26 is to find safety and salvation in the true rock, Jesus. As David said, "…lead me to that rock that is higher than I."[85] The message of the locusts in Proverbs 30:27 is to realise the power of unity. This is followed by the message of the spider in Proverbs 30:28:

---

[85] Psalm 61:2 (NIV)

The spider taketh hold with her hands, and is in kings' palaces.

Proverbs 30:28 (KJV)

Even though great pains are taken to keep spiders out of palaces, they are still found there. They simply keep taking hold with their hands, and they do not give up because of difficulty, resistance or trouble. A spider never gives up and neither should we. It may not be easy, but we need to keep praying at all times and keep on doing the good work that we are called to do. As the idiom says, 'keep on keeping on'. Or as Paul says:

Let us not become weary in doing good, for at the proper time we will reap a harvest if we do not give up.

Galatians 6:9 (NIV)

Therefore, my beloved brothers, be steadfast, immovable, always abounding in the work of the Lord, knowing that in the Lord your labor is not in vain.

1 Corinthians 15:58 (ESV)

Are you willing to learn the lessons some of God's seemingly insignificant creatures can teach us? The artistry of the spider's web design is a microscopic engineering marvel – stand back and admire one today. Then remember to be diligent, tenacious and determined. Take hold of God's promises and refuse to quit.

14

Tracking Spiritual Fitness

Establish my footsteps in Your word...

Psalm 119:133 (NASB)

Everywhere we turn, fitness is all the rage. The newest twist on the trend is keeping track of our personal fitness. Reaching ten thousand steps a day seems to be the epitome of wellness goals these days, especially when everyone is flashing their Fitbit stats in your face. Nifty new technology allows us to monitor our fitness levels. Using your phone as a pedometer or fitness tracker is an easy way to track your steps each day. Having downloaded the app on my phone three months ago I have been pushing myself to hit ten thousand steps a day (about five miles). With this held up as the benchmark of an active lifestyle, it is a healthy outlet for our innate competitiveness as a family. We compare our fitness records at the end of the week and adjust our step goals accordingly. Some days I get a reminder on the phone to be more active – I've been stationary too long!

What if I wore a spiritual fitness tracker? Would it too warn me that I need to be more active and less of a spiritual couch potato? Spiritual growth doesn't just happen, I have to spend time actually 'training' – reading, seeking, meditating and talking to God. Paul instructed Timothy to keep spiritually fit in 1 Timothy 4:7:

Exercise thyself rather unto godliness.

1 Timothy 4:7 (KJV)

J.B. Phillips translates it:

Take time and trouble to keep yourselves spiritually fit.

1 Timothy 4:7 (PHI)

Paul goes on to tell Timothy that "while bodily training is of some value, godliness is of value in every way, as it holds promise for the present life and also for the life to come."[86]

Godliness comes from the old English word 'Godlikeness' which means to have the character and attitude of God. Paul said, "Train yourself." Timothy was personally responsible for his progress in godliness. I discovered that having the fitness tracker on my phone does not take the steps for me! I had to discipline myself to get up and move. Likewise Paul is saying that to train ourselves unto godliness we need to be diligent and disciplined, not sporadic in our doing. Are we being intentional regarding the things of God and showing consistency and commitment? Are we being as proactive with our spiritual fitness as we are with our physical fitness? Do we need a daily reminder to step it up and step it out? Are we keeping in step with the Spirit? To whom shall we go the extra mile to serve?

We are told:

> The steps of a good man are ordered by the LORD: and he delighteth in his way
>
> *Psalm 37:23 (KJV)*

> Establish my footsteps in Your word...
>
> *Psalm 119:133 (NASB)*

Let us intentionally intensify our daily intake of God's Word and allow Him to order our steps. Let's get more active on our spiritual journey.

---

[86] 1 Timothy 4:8 (ESV)

15

The Magazine Stand

Surely he has borne our griefs
and carried our sorrows;
yet we esteemed him stricken,
smitten by God, and afflicted.
But he was pierced for our transgressions;
he was crushed for our iniquities;
upon him was the chastisement that brought us peace,
and with his wounds we are healed.

Isaiah 53:4-5 (ESV)

*M*y last pitstop before boarding my plane was the magazine rack. A browse through some glossy pages usually helped pass the time while cramped in a confined space. I have noticed the plethora of magazine choices has grown in recent years: photography, sport, car, beauty, boating, fishing, wildlife, cross-stitch, gardening, music, science, health and well-being. The 'health and well-being' section has especially skyrocketed lately, with headlines telling us what to ditch or what to do for a more improved lifestyle.

Imagine reading the headline "peace, well-being, healed, made whole". That sounds appealing and is in reality attainable. Isaiah wrote those words in chapter 53 when speaking about Jesus.

But He was wounded for our transgressions, He was bruised
for our guilt and iniquities; the chastisement [needful to
obtain] peace and well-being for us was upon Him, and with
the stripes [that wounded] Him we are healed and made
whole.

Isaiah 53:5 (AMPC)

Peace, well-being, healed, made whole. Our peace was procured by His "chastisement". He Himself paid the heavy and terrible price for our wholeness. "Upon him was the chastisement that brought us peace."

Notice the words in verse 4, "He has borne … and carried our sorrows," "He was pierced," "He was crushed…" The emphasis is on the pronoun 'He'. *He* has made peace and wellbeing possible for us. When Mel Gibson's *The Passion of the Christ* was released, people complained that the scourging scene was too graphic and violent. The truth is that it portrayed only a fraction of what our Lord really suffered on our behalf.

Upon Him was the chastisement that brought us peace. The Hebrew word for peace is *shalom*, which comes from the root verb *shalam*, meaning 'to be complete, perfect and full'. *Shalom* signifies a sense of well-being and harmony both within and without – completeness, wholeness, peace, health, welfare, safety, soundness, tranquility, prosperity, fullness, rest, harmony; the absence of agitation or discord, a state of calm without anxiety or stress, according to the *Old Testament Hebrew Lexical Dictionary*.

In Psalm 35:27 God takes delight in the *shalom* (the wholeness, the total well-being) of His servant. I confess that I bought the health and well-being magazine at the airport stand but I found that true wellbeing does not come from a magazine – it comes from the Messiah, the Prince of Peace.

16

Cows With Names

"Do not fear, for I have redeemed you;
I have summoned you by name; you are mine."

Isaiah 43:1 (NIV)

The average cow can produce about a hundred glasses of milk each day. However, it was only while watching the news last night that I discovered that cows with names produce more milk than those animals who are not named, according to latest research. Cows called Ermintrude, Daisy, Bessie or Lady Moo produce over 450 pints more each year than cows with no names. In a study which surveyed 516 dairy farmers in the UK, Dr Catherine Douglas and Dr Peter Rowlinson at Newcastle University found that treating the animals as individuals increased production. The average amount of milk produced by a cow over its annual ten-month lactation period is 13,198 pints (7,500 litres). Those cows with names had an average higher milk yield of 454 pints (258 litres). Just as people respond better to the personal touch, cows also feel happier and more relaxed if they are given a bit more one-to-one attention.

Every day, month after month, a lactating cow is expected to let down her milk under the expectant eyes of a farmer whose bottom line depends on how much of it he can squeeze out. Elevated stress hormones like cortisol reduce milk production by interfering with the milk-boosting hormone oxytocin. If the cow is more relaxed by calling her name and given a bit more one-to-one attention, she yields more milk. Nearly half of the five hundred farmers surveyed named their cows.

Jesus said:

...the sheep hear his voice: and he calleth his own sheep by
name, and leadeth them out.

John 10:3 (KJV)

Then he told the disciples:

I am the Good Shepherd, and know my sheep, and am known of mine.

John 10:14 (KJV)

He knows His sheep – not the flock, but the sheep. He knows each one by name. That is why the Lord says in the parable of the lost sheep:

"Suppose one of you has a hundred sheep and loses one of them. Doesn't he leave the ninety-nine in the open country and go after the lost sheep until he finds it?"

Luke 15:4 (NIV)

The obvious answer is *yes!* He will! And the amazing thing about this is that, despite the large number – a hundred sheep – the Shepherd will know that one is missing. Why? Because He does not look at the flock, but the sheep. Every one matters. Every one is precious.

God said:

"Do not fear, for I have redeemed you; I have summoned you by name; you are mine."

Isaiah 43:1 (NIV)

Again He stated:

"Can a mother forget her nursing child?
  Can she feel no love for a child she has borne?
But even if that were possible,
  I would never forget you!
See, I have engraved your name on the palms of my hands."

Isaiah 49:15-16 (NLT)

God loves you immensely.[87] He thinks about you all the time[88] and He knows your name.[89] May such knowledge bring peace to your life and may you be productive in His service yielding fruit, more fruit and much fruit[90] to the glory of His name.

---

[87] See John 3:16
[88] See Psalm 139:17-18
[89] See John 10:3
[90] See John 15:8

17

It's More Than a Fabric Conditioner

Praise be to the God and Father of our Lord Jesus Christ, the Father of compassion and the God of all comfort, who comforts us in all our troubles, so that we can comfort those in any trouble with the comfort we ourselves receive from God.

2 Corinthians 1:3-4 (NIV)

*I*t's not just the name of a fabric conditioner. 'Comfort', according to the dictionary means 'to lessen the sadness or sorrow of someone and to strengthen by inspiring with hope and restoring a cheerful outlook'. We derive our English word from the Old French word *conforter* meaning 'to comfort, to solace; to help, strengthen'), and from the Latin verb *confortare* ('to strengthen much') and the noun *comfortis:* from *com-* (expressing intensive force) and *fortis* ('strong').

com + *fortis* = with strength

The Bible tells us that God is the God of all comfort.

"I, even I, am He who comforts you."

Isaiah 51:12 (AMP)

"As a mother comforts her child, so will I comfort you."

Isaiah 66:13 (NIV)

The root meaning of that Hebrew word for comfort is 'to sigh'. You remember when as a child you were running too quickly and you tripped. You scratched your knee and you ran to your mother. Your mother lifted you up onto her knee, and she said, "Now, now; it'll be alright." That's what this verse is saying: "As you sigh, I'll sigh with you." But God not only sighs with us, He strengthens us and we see that in the New Testament book of 2 Corinthians.

Paul's classic passage on comfort is 2 Corinthians 1. God is the author of comfort and "comforts us in all our troubles, so that we can comfort those in any trouble with the comfort we ourselves have received from God"[91]. The Greek word for "comfort" here is *paraklesis*. It literally refers to one who is called alongside to help, support and strengthen. Notice that the word "comforts" is in the present tense. This encouragement is ever-present. He comforts us in all our troubles day by day. Paul wasn't pontificating with pious words from an insulated ivory tower or as an out-of-touch theologian who himself never encountered trial or tragedy. He knew what it was like to endure "affliction"[92]. He said, "We were under great pressure, far beyond our ability to endure, so that we despaired of life itself."[93] So when Paul describes God as the Father of all comfort, he knows first-hand that God comforts us in all our troubles.

I love the TLB translation:

> *What a wonderful God we have – He is the Father of our Lord Jesus Christ, the source of every mercy, and the one who so wonderfully comforts and strengthens us in our hardships and trials. And why does He do this? So that when others are troubled, needing our sympathy and encouragement, we can pass on to them this same help and comfort God has given us.*
>
> *2 Corinthians 1:3-4 (TLB)*

Anyone needing your sympathy and encouragement today? Go ahead – sigh with them and strengthen them as God has strengthened you.

---

[91] 2 Corinthians 1:4 (NIV)
[92] 2 Corinthians 1:8 (NASB)
[93] 2 Corinthians 1:8 (NIV)

18

You Did It for Me

"The King will answer and say to them, 'I assure you and most solemnly say to you, to the extent that you did it for one of these brothers of Mine, even the least of them, you did it for Me.'"

Matthew 25:40 (AMP)

*J*esus said, "You did it for Me." Previous to this He had stated, "For I was hungry, and you gave Me something to eat; I was thirsty, and you gave Me something to drink; I was a stranger, and you invited Me in."[94]

"The righteous asked Him, 'Lord, when did we see You hungry, and feed You, or thirsty, and give You something to drink? And when did we see You as a stranger, and invite You in, or naked, and clothe You? And when did we see You sick, or in prison, and come to You?'"

Matthew 25:37-39 (NKJV)

Jesus replied in verse 40, "...to the extent that you did it for one of these brothers of Mine, even the least of them, you did it for Me."

The words of Matthew 25 give definition and direction to our Christian action. We don't have to look too far to find the people whom Jesus identified here. They are all around us in society today. But what are we doing to help? An unknown author in a poignant poem has captured eloquently the way in which we so religiously fall short of Christ's demand of service for others. It says:

I was hungry and you formed a committee to investigate my hunger.
I was homeless and you filed a report on my plight.

---

[94] Matthew 25:35 (AMP)

I was sick and you held a seminar on the situation of the underprivileged.
You investigated all aspects of my plight and yet I am still hungry, homeless and sick.

Author unknown

Sadly, to some Jesus had to say:

"'I was hungry, and you gave Me nothing to eat; I was thirsty, and you gave Me nothing to drink...'"

Matthew 25:42 (AMP)

William Barclay (1907-1978), biblical scholar and theologian, said this:

If we had known it was you, we would gladly have helped. But we thought it was only some common man who wasn't worth helping. It is still true that there are those who will help if they are given praise and thanks and publicity. But to help like that is not to help, it is to pander to self-esteem. Such help is not generosity; it is disguised selfishness. The help which wins the approval of God is that which is given for nothing but the sake of helping.

Martin Luther declared:

The world does not need a definition of religion as much as it needs a demonstration.

Consider the following Scriptures to spur us into action today:

Show yourself in all respects a model of good deeds.

Titus 2:7 (NRSV)

Do not withhold good from those to whom it is due, when it is in your power to do it. Do not say to your neighbour, "Go and come again, tomorrow I will give it" – when you have it with you.

Proverbs 3:27-28 (ESV)

If a brother or sister is ill-clad and in lack of daily food, and one of you says to them, 'Go in peace, be warmed and filled,' without giving them the things needed for the body, what does it profit?

James 2:15-16 (RSV)

Remember that whatever you do, at the end of the day Jesus says, "You did it for Me."

19

Pruning Roses: When to Make the Cut

"Every branch that does bear fruit He prunes, that it may bear more fruit."

John 15:2 (ESV)

"*P*runing Roses: When to Make the Cut." This was a newspaper caption which caught my attention. Outside my front door I have a number of rose bushes which delight visitors with their vibrant colour and fragrance in the summer months. People ask me what I do to get such beautiful blooms year after year and I have to tell them the truth: I ignore them except for their annual cut-back when my husband runs along them with the chain saw on the first available day off after Christmas!

Pruning, whether from an accomplished rose pruner or an amateur like myself, can help plants to grow to their optimum. The act of cutting a rose branch helps the plant to produce a hormone called auxin. This growth hormone is present in the main stem of most plants and pruning sends it to the freshly cut stem and encourages it to produce new shoots. Pruning encourages new growth and bloom and removes dead wood.

We see from today's passage that God prunes us, His branches, so that "we may bear more fruit". He removes the deadwood, the dead branches and suckers which are draining away our spiritual vitality. In verse 8 He says:

"By this my Father is glorified, that you bear much fruit and so prove to be my disciples."

John 15:8 (ESV)

The Greek verb translated as "prune" is *kathairō*, meaning 'to cleanse of filth and impurity, to prune trees and vines from useless shoots'. God's pruning is not meant to hurt us, it is meant to purge us of the things that are keeping us from operating at full capacity for the Lord. God's Word is the perfect tool for pruning us. It is disconnecting us from the overgrowth of apathy and complacency, negative talk, self-centredness and impatience with others. It is the cutting off of pride, fear, ungodly traits and attitudes. God's Word is sharp so that it can remove the unwanted 'branches' in our lives without harming us. Hebrews 4:12 says that the Word of God is "alive, and active, and sharper than any two-edged sword, piercing even to the division of soul and spirit, of joints and marrow, and able to judge the thoughts and intents of the heart."[95] God also knows the perfect time to prune us.

Let us submit to the secateurs of Scripture knowing there is purpose in our pruning. May we be fruitful and flourish bringing glory to God.

---

[95] Hebrews 4:12 (MEV)

20

Truthing in Love

Instead, speaking the truth in love, we will grow to become in every respect the mature body of him who is the head, that is, Christ.

Ephesians 4:15 (NIV)

*I*f you look at the original language of Ephesians 4:15, you will be surprised to see that the word for "speaking" is not there. Instead, Paul takes the word 'truth' and makes it into a verb. So literally, the verse reads, "But truthing in love, we are to grow up in all aspects into Him." Of course, 'truthing' isn't an actual English word – but let's pretend it is for a moment; it'll help us understand the phrase better. "Speaking the truth" is a translation of the single Greek word *aleuthontes*. About this word, theologian John Stott said:

"Speaking the truth in love" is not the best rendering of his expression, for the Greek verb makes no reference to our speech. Literally, it means, "truthing in love" and includes the notions of "maintaining," "living" and "doing the truth."[96]

Strong's Concordance states:

I say (speak) truth, do truth, maintain truth (the truth).

This comes out in the Amplified Bible's translation:

Rather, let our lives lovingly express truth [in all things, speaking truly, dealing truly, living truly]. Enfolded in love, let us grow up in every way and in all things into Him Who is the Head, [even] Christ (the Messiah, the Anointed One).

Ephesians 4:15 (AMPC)

---

[96] John Stott; *Reading Ephesians with John Stott: 11 Weeks for Individuals or Groups;* ISBN 9780830831951

The verse is not saying that we should simply speak the truth, but that we should live out the truth in both word and action. Speaking is just one small application of its meaning. Another way to translate the idea behind this phrase might be 'displaying the truth in love'. Paul also used a present participle of the verb to indicate that the 'truthing' is to be continuous. So, with truth in view, this verb indicates ongoing truthfulness as a way of life.

There is a need for equilibrium between what is spoken and what is lived out. May our lives lovingly express truth in all things. As we share the gospel, may we do so in a loving way. As we interact with others on social media, may we first ask ourselves, "Am I truthing in love?" As we carry out our day-to-day business, again we need to ensure that we are speaking truly, dealing truly and living truly.

21

The Heavens are Telling

The heavens declare the glory of God;
* the skies proclaim the work of his hands.*
Day after day they pour forth speech;
* night after night they display knowledge.*
There is no speech or language
* where their voice is not heard.*
Their voice goes out into all the earth,
* their words to the ends of the world.*
In the heavens he has pitched a tent for the sun,
* which is like a bridegroom coming forth from his pavilion,*
* like a champion rejoicing to run his course.*
It rises at one end of the heavens
* and makes its circuit to the other;*
* nothing is hidden from its heat.*

Psalm 19:1-6 (NIV)

The Creation (German: *Die Schöpfung*) is an oratorio written in 1797 by Joseph Haydn and is considered to be one of his finest works. It celebrates the creation of the world as described in the Book of Genesis and was first performed in Vienna in 1799. Psalm 19:1 provides the opening words for its well-known chorus: "The heavens are telling the glory of God."[97]

The following truths are found in these verses.

- *God's glory is being proclaimed.* The sky is preaching the glory of God every day. The wonders of creation are meant to be billboards advertising God's glory, showing us a glimpse of the order and beauty of the Creator. The Message Bible (MSG) puts it, "God's glory is on tour in the skies."

---

[97] TLB

- *The testimony is constant.* This revelation about God's majesty and glory is constant, occurring "day after day" and "night after night". We are constantly reminded of God's existence. There is never a silent moment during day or night when creation ceases to pour forth and breathe out its unified witness to God's glory. When David says that the heavens "pour forth" this message, the word he uses for "pour forth" speaks of an artesian well, or a geyser that unfailingly sends a cascade of hot water shooting into the air, or a fresh spring bubbling forth, never running dry. They are flooding the world day by day.
- *It is worldwide in scope.* The scope of this testimony is worldwide. All people, everywhere, have access to this form of God's revelation. There are no geographic barriers.
- *There is no language barrier.* Since this is a non-verbal form of communication, there is no language barrier. All people, in every language, are able to comprehend this form of God revealing Himself.

Remember that this beautiful display of nature is to point us to God Himself. As John Piper pointed out:

> *The glory of creation and the glory of God are as different as the love poem and the love, the painting and the landscape, the ring and the marriage. It would be a great folly and a great tragedy if a man loved his wedding band more than he loved his bride.*[98]

Take time to appreciate God afresh today.

---

[98] Piper; *The Pleasures of God* (1991); pp.86-87

22

Poured Prayers

Trust in him at all times, you people;
pour out your hearts to Him,
for God is our refuge.

Psalm 62:8 (NIV)

*O*ur prayers are the verbal expression of our faith. There are many ways in which the Bible refers to prayer. It is called:

- bowing the knees;

For this cause I bow my knees unto the Father of our Lord Jesus Christ.

Ephesians 3:14 (KJV)

- lifting up the soul;

Unto thee, O LORD, do I lift up my soul.

Psalm 25:1 (KJV)

- seeking the face of the Lord;

Seek the LORD and His strength;
seek His face continually.

1 Chronicles 16:11 (NASB)

- crying for help;

Hear my cry for help, my King and my God, for to you I pray.

Psalm 5:2 (NIV)

- lifting up your voice.

They lifted up their voice to God with one accord.

Acts 4:24 (KJV)

One of my favourite expressions for prayer is found in Psalm 62:8 where it instructs us to, "Pour out your hearts to Him."

> *Trust in him at all times, you people,*
>   *pour out your hearts to Him,*
>   *for God is our refuge…*
>
>

Psalm 62:8 (NIV)

Spurgeon said:

> *Turn the vessel of your soul upside down in his secret presence, and let your inmost thoughts, desires, sorrows, and sins be poured out like water.*

We are given a good example in 1 Samuel 1:13-15 with Hannah pouring out her heart to God.

> *And Hannah answered and said, No, my lord, I am a woman of a sorrowful spirit: I have drunk neither wine nor strong drink, but have poured out my soul before the LORD.*
>
>

1 Samuel 1:15 (KJV)

The Hebrew in this case says that she merely spoke her heart (the word *debar* is used). However, in Psalm 62:8 David is not saying to solely speak your heart to God but to *shaphak* your heart to God. The word *shaphak* is the word for melting wax and pouring it into a mould. David says that we need to melt and pour our hearts out to God. David realised that God alone was the one he could count on. When we face difficulties, we may talk with friends and family members, but God wants us to remember to pour out our hearts to Him. This involves spending time with Him, being confident in our relationship with Him, sharing with Him every detail of our needs – every thought, every feeling, every concern. God is not looking for polished prayers but poured prayers.

We are told in Lamentations:

> *"Arise, cry aloud in the night*
> *At the beginning of the night watches;*
> *Pour out your heart like water*
> *Before the presence of the Lord;*
> *Lift up your hands to Him*
> *For the life of your little ones*

Who are faint because of hunger
At the head of every street."

Lamentations 2:19 (NASB)

Will you pour out your heart to God today? Tell Him everything that's hurting you. He cares. He's waiting to take that burden from you and exchange it for His peace.

23

Avoiding Capture

Don't let anyone capture you with empty philosophies and high-sounding nonsense that come from human thinking and from the spiritual powers of this world, rather than from Christ.

Colossians 2:8 (NLT)

ecently I was watching a nature mini-series called *Animals With Cameras*. If the name doesn't give it away, *Animals With Cameras* employed state-of-the-art cameras worn by animals themselves. The role of these animal cinematographers was to help expand human understanding of their habitats and behaviour. The series featured an all-star cast of animals, including meerkats, cheetahs, bears, and fur seals. The series was amazing, but the fascinating part for me was watching the crew trying to fit the cameras onto the meerkats, most of which were adept at avoiding capture. It's amazing how alert they are and how quickly they can move their heads as a camera collar approaches.

When Paul wrote, "Don't let anyone capture you," the term he used referred to taking captives in war and leading them away as booty. He was saying, "Don't let anybody kidnap you." We are in danger of being kidnapped by error. The warning against being taken captive is a present, active, singular participle showing that the danger is ever-present. The KJV has an interesting take: "Beware lest any man spoil you."

What is the manner in which we can be taken "captive"? The answer Paul gives is: "...empty philosophies and high-sounding nonsense that come from human thinking." There are many philosophies packaged attractively and marketed aggressively today, each incompatible with the Christian faith and dedicated to subverting it. Their origin is man or human thinking. They arise out of the thinking of men, find a foothold in society, and then are passed along from generation to generation so as to appear popular and widely supported. It is, in Paul's words, "not according to Christ".

Everything we learn needs to be sifted through the grid of the question, "Is it according to Christ?" That is to say, if it is in any way contrary to the revelation of God in Christ or diminishes from his supremacy and glory, it is to be shunned. J.B. Phillips' New Testament translation states:

> *Be careful that nobody spoils your faith through intellectualism or high-sounding nonsense. Such stuff is at best founded on men's ideas of the nature of the world and disregards Christ!*
>
> *Colossians 2:8 (PHI)*

Avoid men's ideas of the nature of the world. Another translation, The Voice, says:

> *Make sure no predator makes you his prey through some misleading philosophy and empty deception based on traditions fabricated by mere mortals. These are sourced in the elementary principles originating in this world and not in the Anointed One (so don't let their talks capture you).*
>
> *Colossians 2:8 (TVT)*

Let's be alert and adept at avoiding capture.

24

Millstone or Milestone?

If you continue in My word, then you are truly disciples of Mine; and you will know the truth, and the truth will make you free.

John 8:31-32 (NASB)

A little girl asked her mother, "Mummy, why do you cut off the ends of the meat before you cook it?" The girl's mother went on to tell her that she thought that cutting off the ends off the meat added flavour by allowing it to better absorb the spices – but perhaps she had better ask her grandma since she had learned it from her. The little girl found her grandmother and asked, "Grandma, why do you and mummy chop off the ends of the meat before you cook it?" Her grandmother answered, "I think it allows the meat to stay tender because it soaks up the juices, but why don't you ask your Nana because I learned from her and she has always done it that way." The little girl was getting a little frustrated, but climbed up in her great-grandmother's lap and asked, "Nana, why do you and Mummy and Grandma cut the ends off of the meat before you cook it?" Nana answered, "I don't know why your Mum and Grandma do it, but I did it because my pot wasn't big enough."

Why do we do what we do? The term 'tradition' renders a Greek word that signifies 'instruction that has been handed down'. What is the source of what you believe? Sometimes traditions can be helpful, other times a hindrance. Some common practices, embalmed by time, become accepted as 'the voice of God'. Such traditions may become burdens,[99] unnecessarily levied upon people, robbing them of legitimate freedom in serving Christ. They become millstones weighting us down rather than milestones celebrating the legacy of the past.

---

[99] See Matthew 23:4

Jesus said that you will know the truth and the truth will make you free. He told us that God's Word is truth:

"Your word is truth."

John 17:17 (NASB)

It is by studying God's infallible Word that we know the Truth. I love the example set by the Bereans in Acts 17:11:

Now these were more noble-minded than those in Thessalonica, for they received the word with great eagerness, examining the Scriptures daily to see whether these things were so.

Acts 17:11 (NASB)

They received the word with great eagerness and examined what they were taught against the litmus test of Scripture. It is by this method that we can be kept in the truth and delivered from error. Pursuing this example avoids the potentially disastrous 'blind leading the blind' syndrome.

Do you lean heavily on tradition? If so, is the tradition rooted in the Truth of God's Word? It is my prayer and hope that the Word of God will dwell within you and you will truly know the Truth and be free indeed.

25

Room 101

There are six things the LORD hates,
  seven that are detestable to him:
haughty eyes,
a lying tongue,
hands that shed innocent blood,
a heart that devises wicked schemes,
feet that are quick to rush into evil,
a false witness who pours out lies
and a person who stirs up conflict in the community.

Proverbs 6:16-19 (NIV)

oom 101 is a comedy television series in which celebrities are invited to discuss their pet hates and persuade the host to consign those hates to oblivion in Room 101. The title *Room 101* is synonymous with the most horrible and frightening place in the world, as created by George Orwell in his dystopian novel *Nineteen Eighty-Four*. So, what should be despatched in Room 101? Some of the previous episodes I watched suggested sniffing, coat hangers, misplaced clapping, lateness, cyclists wearing lycra and queuing as examples of pet peeves which should be banished into Room 101.

Supposing you could consign your grievances to Room 101 – what would they be? In Proverbs 6:16-19 God shares a list of things He hates. What does God hate?

Heading up the list is "haughty eyes." What are "haughty eyes"? They are eyes that look down on others in a condescending way. The expression 'looking down our nose' at someone applies here. The Amplified Bible puts it:

A proud look [the spirit that makes one overestimate himself and underestimate others].

Proverbs 6:17 (AMPC)

Pride is putting ourselves on a pedestal above others. Haughty eyes make a person overestimate himself and underestimate others in terms of spirituality, knowledge, intellect etc. Such people are arrogant, unteachable, rebellious and judgmental. Over and over again, we are told in the Scriptures that God resists the proud. God resists all who are proud and gives grace only to those who are humble.[100]

> *Humble yourselves in the sight of the Lord, and He shall lift you up.*
>
> *James 4:10 (KJV)*

When we begin to think of ourselves more highly and with unparalleled importance, we are forgetting the fact that anything good in us is the result of Christ living in us and the grace we have received. As we go about our day remember Romans 12:3 tells us:

> *Do not think of yourself more highly than you ought, but rather think of yourself with sober judgment...*
>
> *Romans 12:3 (NIV)*

Philippians 2:3 advises:

> *Do nothing out of selfish ambition or vain conceit. Rather, in humility value others above yourselves.*
>
> *Philippians 2:3 (NIV)*

As far as we are concerned, let's consign haughty eyes to Room 101.

---

[100] See James 4:6

26

Stay on Track

You're blessed when you stay on course, walking steadily on the road revealed by God.

Psalm 119:1 (MSG)

The Rev. W. Awdry first published the book *Thomas the Tank Engine* in 1945. Since then it has become a popular TV series for children. Thomas the Tank Engine is a steam train which puffs allow his branch line and gets into all kinds of adventures and situations with the other engines. He is easy to spot as he is a blue locomotive and has a number 1 painted on his side. Having watched many episodes over the years with my children, I have noticed something about Thomas: he thinks that the rails confine him and imagines that getting off the rails is the way to freedom.

In life, many have the same mentality, thinking they know better (as if they have an invisible number 1 on their side too and are unwilling to submit to a conductor). Yet true freedom is found when we stay connected with God and run along the tracks He has for us. I recall one scene which pictures Thomas on his side, having fallen off the train tracks. He is shouting, "I'm free! I'm free at last. I've fallen off the rails and I'm free!" Of course, the reality is that Thomas is far freer when his wheels are on the rails and he is operating in line with how he has been created to function.

Trust GOD from the bottom of your heart;
   don't try to figure out everything on your own.
Listen for GOD's voice in everything you do, everywhere you go;
   He's the one who will keep you on track.

Proverbs 3:5-6 (MSG)

The rails are the key to freedom. When we conduct our lives along the precepts God has laid down for us, we are truly free. Jesus said:

> ... *"If you continue in My word, then you are truly disciples of Mine; and you will know the truth, and the truth will make you free."*
>
> *John 8:31-32 (NASB)*

The key is to "continue in my word". Don't derail! It is for freedom that Christ has set us free.[101] Determine to stay on God's tracks. Don't let anything or anyone derail you.

---

[101] See Galatians 5:1

27

The Land of Nod

When you lie down, you will not be afraid;
When you lie down, your sleep will be sweet.

Proverbs 3:24 (AMP)

At some stage you have probably heard reference to the 'Land of Nod'. It is used to refer to the state of sleep or an imaginary land of sleep. We also could say that someone is 'nodding off', especially in a sitting position. The Land of Nod has been used to refer to sleep since the 18th century, notably by Irish satirist Jonathan Swift in *Polite Conversation:* "I'm going to the Land of Nod." The association with sleep developed because of the word 'nod', an involuntary movement of the head when falling asleep, but what is the original meaning of the expression 'the Land of Nod'?

The very first few pages of the Bible refer to the Land of Nod, and locate it "east of Eden"[102]. It is where Cain dwelt after being cast out by God after murdering his brother Abel. The Bible says that he "went out from the presence of the Lord and dwelt in the land of Nod" [103]. It was originally a place of anguished exile rather than of peaceful sleep. *Nod* is the Hebrew root for 'wandering' and has connotations of restlessness and trembling. The noun *Nod* in Hebrew means 'wanderer, exile or fugitive'. This corresponds to God's word to Cain that he would "be a fugitive and a wanderer on the earth."[104]

Perhaps you have had nights when you lay down to sleep but your mind was restless, your thoughts were swirling and anxieties pressing hard. If so, consider the following Scriptures:

---

[102] Genesis 4:16 (NKJV)
[103] Ibid.
[104] Genesis 4:12 (ESV)

When you lie down, you will not be afraid;
When you lie down, your sleep will be sweet.

Proverbs 3:24 (AMP)

Your sleep shall be sweet. That word "sweet" means 'free of all uneasy thoughts and cares, sound and refreshing, pleasant and comfortable'. Spurgeon said, "When we go to bed at night, let this word smooth our pillow."

In peace I will both lie down and sleep;
for you alone, O LORD, make me dwell in safety.

Psalm 4:8 (ESV)

For He gives to His beloved sleep.

Psalm 127:2 (ESV)

We can trust in God and sleep even when we face the storms of life, just as Jesus and Peter did in the following verses:

But He was ... asleep on a pillow. And they awoke Him and said to Him, "Teacher, do You not care that we are perishing?"

Mark 4:38 (NKJV)

And when Herod was about to bring him out, that night Peter was sleeping, bound with two chains between two soldiers.

Acts 12:6 (NKJV)

May you lay down tonight free of all uneasy thoughts and cares and may your sleep be sound and refreshing.

28

Why We Sigh

Lord, all my desire is before You; and my sighing is not hidden from You.

Psalm 38:9 (AMPC)

On a visit to Venice I had the privilege of seeing what's known as Ponte dei Sospiri, or 'Bridge of Sighs'. The bridge passes over the Rio di Palazzo and connects the Dogi's palace to the Prigioni, the prisons built across the canal in the late sixteenth century. It apparently received its name because prisoners would sigh at their final view of beautiful Venice through the window before being taken down to their cells.

What is a sigh and why do we sigh? A sigh, a deep long breath about twice the volume of a typical breath, can express emotions we cannot put into words. A sigh can also serve as a sort of stretch for your lungs – a periodic deep breath inflates the alveoli, tiny sacs in the lungs where oxygen and carbon dioxide pass in and out of the blood. Various stimuli can trigger a sigh. The trilling of a phone, particularly the office phone. The thud of bills through the letterbox. Whether it's a sigh of relief, or a sigh of grief, we all sigh throughout the day. The average person sighs every five minutes – or about twelve times an hour.

A lot can be wrapped up in a sigh. I often let out sighs after moving a heavy bag of groceries, or laying my head down on my pillow at the end of a tiring day, or when I try to communicate clearly to someone only to be misunderstood. Psalm 38:9 reminds us that nothing is filtered from God. He hears your sighs of exhaustion, exasperation, despair and anguish. They may go unnoticed by others, but God hears them like a heartbeat. Today, all you may be able to do is sigh, but know that is not hidden from our Lord. Just as parents can read slightest sighs of their children and can tell when something is troubling them, so God knows the story behind our slightest sigh.

Psalm 38 was written in a time of deep anguish and exhaustion. David wrote:

I am bent over and greatly bowed down.

Psalm 38:6 (AMP)

I groan because of the disquiet and moaning of my heart.

Psalm 38:8 (AMP)

My heart throbs violently, my strength fails me.

Psalm 38:10 (AMP)

In the centre of this psalm David says:

All my longings lie open before you, Lord;
my sighing is not hidden from you.

Psalm 38:9 (NIV)

He knew God was intimately acquainted with his pain and understood his sighing. That's why the psalm concludes with the words:

Make haste to help me, O Lord, my Salvation.

Psalm 38:22 (KJV)

We read in Exodus:

And the children of Israel sighed by reason of the bondage.

Exodus 2:23 (KJV)

Their sighing expressed their suffering and sorrow under the oppression of their Egyptian taskmasters. Again God heard their sighs. In Psalm 12:5 God says:

...for the sighing of the needy, now will I arise, saith the LORD.

Psalm 12:5 (KJV)

God responds to the sighing of His people. "Now I will arise," He says. May that word encourage us today and fill us with hope.

29

No Flies on Us

*Then the LORD said to Moses, "Go to Pharaoh and say to him,
'This is what the LORD says: Let my people go, so that they
may worship me.'"*

Exodus 8:1 (NIV)

We have all heard that old joke, "Waiter, what's this fly doing in my soup?" "Um, looks to me to be backstroke, sir." Flies in reality are little to laugh about and can be noisome nuisances, especially in summer when we leave the windows open. I'm told that flies have terrible vision despite the fact that they have over four thousands lenses per eye. Yet when I go to swat one, the ultra-nimble fly seems to be the Ferrari of the insect world.

In Exodus 8 we read of the fourth plague where flies were not only found in the Egyptians' soup, but everywhere.

*Dense swarms of flies poured into Pharaoh's palace and into
the houses of his officials; throughout Egypt the land was
ruined by the flies.*

Exodus 8:24 (NIV)

The Hebrew phrase translated "swarms of flies" is literally rendered 'a mixture of noisome beasts'. Psalm 78:45 tells us:

*He sent divers sorts of flies among them, which devoured
them...*

Psalm 78:45 (KJV)

God told Moses to go before Pharaoh and tell him to, "Let my people go, so they may worship me." God wanted His people to travel three days' journey into the wilderness and sacrifice to Him there. Exact instructions were given and were meant to be obeyed. Although Pharaoh did not want to let them go, he did offer some compromises. You say, how noble! Not at all. It's Satan's old, deceptive trickery – mingling truth with error. Three times Pharaoh tried to get Moses to compromise in the message and manner in which Israel was to worship God. After the plague of flies, Pharaoh says to Moses:

Go ye and sacrifice to your God in the land.

Exodus 8:25 (KJV)

Did you catch it? The compromise is very subtle. Go sacrifice to God, but stay here in Egypt. 'Stay in Egypt' was his compromise. Yet God specifically wanted them to travel three days' journey into the wilderness to worship and separate themselves from Egypt. Multitudes, like Pharaoh, vainly imagine that God will accept them today on their terms. He will not. He demands complete surrender. Moses said, "We cannot serve our God according to your rules."

His first compromise firmly repulsed, Pharaoh resorts to another, even more subtle. Notice his next move. He says:

"I will let you go ... [but] not ... very far away."

Exodus 8:28 (ESV)

This is just as much a compromise as being in Egypt proper, yet many have bought that lie. He knew that if the Israelites were not far away, he would still be able to recapture them easily. God didn't just want Israel to be 'not very far away' from Egypt – He wanted them out of Egypt altogether! For us to grow to spiritual maturity as children of God, He desires to wean us from our sense of dependency upon the things of this world. The kingdom of God is not of this world. Moses no more conceded to Pharaoh's second suggestion than he did the first, and neither should we. Have we separated from the world – but not very far away?

In chapter 10 after a play of locusts, Pharaoh again seeks a compromise. He says:

"Have only the men go and worship the LORD."

Exodus 10:11 (NIV)

In other words, "Go, but don't take your families. Leave the next generation in Egypt, ignorant of God's ways!" This portion of Scripture is instructive for us as the enemy still uses the same tricks to cause us to compromise our faith today. Beware the subtlety of compromise. Compromise with the world – however much it may be dressed up – robs us of our blessing and is dishonouring to God. At every stage of negotiations with Pharaoh, Moses consistently rejected any concession or compromise. May we likewise be faithful lest the enemy get the advantage.

30

Long Life

...for length of days and years of life and peace they will add to you.

Proverbs 3:2 (ESV)

*J*uan Ponce de León (1474-1521) was a Spanish explorer and conquistador remembered for his search for the legendary Fountain of Youth, a spring which restores youth to whoever drinks from it or bathes in it. If you ask anyone about ageing, they'll probably tell you they want to live a long and healthy life. Many people today spend much money, time and energy in an attempt to lengthen their lives. Our National Anthem says, "God save our gracious Queen! Long live our noble Queen!"

In Proverbs 3:2 we are told that when we walk in the ways and statutes of God and apply them, our welfare is affected.

> *For length of days and years of life [worth living] and tranquility and prosperity [the wholeness of life's blessings] they will add to you.*

Proverbs 3:2 (AMP)

"*...length of days...* " The expression is literally 'extension of days', and signifies the prolongation of life. The psalmist asked:

> *Who is the man who desires life*
> *And loves length of days that he may see good?*

Psalm 34:12 (NASB)

> *The fear of the LORD is the beginning of wisdom,*
>   *and the knowledge of the Holy One is understanding.*
> *For by me your days will be multiplied,*
>   *and years of life will be added to you.*

Proverbs 9:10-11 (ESV)

"Because he loves me," says the LORD, "I will rescue him,
I will protect him, for he acknowledges my name. ...
With long life I will satisfy him
and show him my salvation."

Psalm 91:14-16 (NIV)

"...years of life..." It literally means 'a life worthwhile living'. We are talking here of not just quantity but quality of life, not just a full lifespan but life to the full. In the future, scientists may be able to prolong life, but will it be worth living? An increased lifespan is of little value unless it is for a life worth living.

"...tranquility and prosperity..." Not only that but "the wholeness of life's blessings". No-one likes to live in a pressure cooker of stress, but peace sounds appealing.

Let the peace of Christ [the inner calm of one who walks daily with Him] be the controlling factor in your hearts [deciding and settling questions that arise].

Colossians 3:15 (AMP)

We can have "the inner calm of one who walks daily with Him".

Take to heart God's Word. Daily walk with Him and make each day count.

31

Keep it Shut

Whoso keepeth his mouth and his tongue keepeth his soul from troubles..

Proverbs 21:23 (KJV)

A number of idioms have developed regarding our mouths. For example, 'be a bigmouth', 'loudmouth', 'put one's foot in one's mouth', 'run off at the mouth', 'shoot one's mouth off', 'speak with a forked tongue' etc... An unbridled tongue is dangerous and can cause trouble.

There is wisdom in keeping our mouths shut. Someone recently shared with me a list (author unknown) containing some simple advice as to when to keep your mouth shut. It quotes twenty occasions:

1. in the heat of anger (Proverbs 14:17);
2. when you don't have all the facts (Proverbs 18:13);
3. when you haven't verified the story (Deuteronomy 17:6);
4. if your words will offend a weaker brother (1 Corinthians 8:11);
5. if your words will be a poor reflection of the Lord or your friends and family (1 Peter 2:21-23);
6. when you are tempted to joke about sin (Proverbs 14:9);
7. when you would be ashamed of your words later (Proverbs 8:8);
8. when you are tempted to make light of holy things (Ecclesiastes 5:2);
9. if your words would convey a wrong impression (Proverbs 17:27);
10. if the issue is none of your business (Proverbs 14:10);
11. when you are tempted to tell an outright lie (Proverbs 4:24);
12. if your words will damage someone's reputation (Proverbs 16:27);
13. if your words will destroy a friendship (Proverbs 25:28);
14. when you are feeling critical (James 3:9);
15. if you can't speak without yelling (Proverbs 25:28);

16. when it is time to listen (Proverbs 13:1);

17. if you may have to eat your words later (Proverbs 18:21);

18. if you have already said it more than once – after that it becomes nagging (Proverbs 19:13);

19. when you are tempted to flatter a wicked person (Proverbs 24:24);

20. when you are supposed to be working instead (Proverbs 14:23).

These Scriptures are not just applicable to our literal mouths and words; they are equally applicable to all the ways we broadcast ourselves, even in social media. Talking too much can get anyone into trouble. I'm sure you have heard the words on television, "You have the right to remain silent. Anything you say can and will be used against you." We are accountable for our words. So, "Watch your tongue and keep your mouth shut, and you will stay out of trouble."

What Shall I Read Next?

Times of Refreshing

AUTUMN DEVOTIONAL

Ruth Gregg

Foreword by Tommy Stewart